DITA ARZT-WEGMAN

DISCOVER THE HIDDEN TREASURES OF SLEEP

Your Soul • Your Dream • Natural Science

Copyright @2020 by Dita Arzt-Wegman

All rights reserved. No part of this book may be reproduced in any form or by any electronic or mechanical means, including information storage and retrieval systems, without permission in writing from the publisher, except by reviewers, who may quote brief passages in a review.

This publication contains the opinions and ideas of its author. It is intended to provide helpful and informative material on the subjects addressed in the publication. The author and publisher specifically disclaim all responsibility for any liability, loss or risk, personal or otherwise, which is incurred as a consequence, directly or indirectly, of the use and application of any of the contents of this book.

WORKBOOK PRESS LLC
187 E Warm Springs Rd,
Suite B285, Las Vegas, NV 89119, USA

Website: https://workbookpress.com/
Hotline: 1-888-818-4856
Email: admin@workbookpress.com

Ordering Information:
Quantity sales. Special discounts are available on quantity purchases by corporations, associations, and others.
For details, contact the publisher at the address above.

ISBN-13:   978-1-954753-54-9 (Paperback Version)
             978-1-954753-55-6 (Digital Version)

REV. DATE: 15/03/2021

DISCOVER THE HIDDEN TREASURES OF SLEEP!

Your Soul - Your Dreams and Natural-Science

...what your Soul gathers from the Cosmos....
...is Knowledge for the World of Tomorrow!

The Power of Planets and Stars
... and how they move us humans!

Astronomy – *"the royal art"* – of Nostradamus

DISCOVER
the
HIDDEN TREASURES OF SLEEP

…..Opens the door to what shall be an extraordinary journey behind the appearances, guiding you into the realm of Spirit / Soul which lies higher in creation than our earth and our body belongs .Gods-Will what is of Spirit is human-beings core ,we have in us , knowing as our Soul we feel from deep within connecting us with the beyond , were the powerful material ,the pulse behind the appearances originate , we enter every night in our subconscious during our different stages of the Sleep-process .

During sleep our Soul sets out on her journey into her finer eternal sphere her region of origin , ,where she can bathe in her atmosphere of snow white purity , beauty and strength to be nourished and thereby gaining strength for our new day to begin *"refreshed "* in order to create in our overall condition a harmonious interaction of Body-Mind and Spirit , like an equilibrium such as in the balancing of scales. ***This is the actual purpose of why we need Sleep !***

This book is not a read. It is a journey separating the mind in its day activity from your soul nourishment during sleep, leading you to the deepest realm of human being's origin, we enter every night connecting with the powerful material subconsciously we need for maintaining our good health, happiness and overall well –being .

Our nocturnal dreams ,intuitively perceived, interpreted by Nostradamus,(by his royal Art of Astronomy) is our open window, like a sneak peek into our tomorrow , letting us know what lies ahead…….

Read on my friends,…..
And *live* your dream !.

TABLE OF CONTENTS

Introduction 1
Sleep–Soul—Dream: what science has to say

Foreword 5

Natural - Science and Nostradamus! 11
... The Cosmos and Dreams

Secrets Of The Universe! 19
It has a beginning but no end...

Discover the Secrets of Sleep 25
Natural Science – Spiritual Purpose!

What Are Dreams? 39
Fantasies or predictive messages?

The New Millennium 130
Turning point for mankind

Planet Earth---Mother Nature 136
Mans' temporary home

Epilogue 147

About The Author 153

Testimonials / Bibliography 157

Appendix 159

Nostradamus His Life and Legacy 161

The Corona Virus 174

INTRODUCTION

In this book we shall explore the interplay between "sleep, soul, and dream". We shall explore how scientists have studied and explained the essential human necessities of "Sleep and Dream". Science studies sleep, sets up sleep clinics, and polysomnography (sleep readings). Science describes the different stages of sleep, and how dreams occur in the phase of REM (rapid-eye-movement) sleep.

But it is fair to say that science is far from perfect, especially as it focuses its investigation and analysis only from the perspective of matter. However, there are two sides to phenomena, the other perspective being the invisible spirit- power behind the manifestation. This awareness necessitates knowledge of the up-building Cosmic Laws. It is an awareness that would show us the interconnectedness of all aspects of life, with the effect visible in all forms of matter which also is affecting us humans in our personal life's journey. Having a foundation of Nature's lawful structure and an understanding of its basic building blocks, only than we can continue to build our personal life on a solid ground, shape our future in a steadfast resistant to any storm; and that will lead us to understand life's purpose and emerge over time in a rounded-up spirit- maturity. The pulse of energy radiation suffusing the cosmos has a core of the spirit; therefore only radiation can generate movement, which is the essence of existence. Science has in recent times acknowledged a *'conscious energy'*, which is the actual invisible substance at the heart of all matter. But the omission to incorporate this 'invisible powerful substance' in scientific research is one of the greatest obstacles to progress in science and to the goal of comprehending the actual core, what makes us human, is (the spirit) the origin and also the true basis of any subject.

Long ago scientists thought that the world was flat, that the earth was the center of the universe, and that Darwin's theory of evolution was the factual narrative of the development of life in the world. Darwin's theory is both right and wrong at the same time when examined from two perspectives.

Galileo, Copernicus, Keppler, to name some of the great minds of humanity, helped disprove flaws harbored by the one-sided narratives of science, which have demonstrated only *'one part of the whole'* and are not efficient at arriving at the foundation that holds the **Truth.**

Since everything that exists has two sides, as I mentioned before, from the perspective of the invisible and the physically visible operating forces, are like connecting threads pulsing through the entire Creation–both perspectives must be taken into account in order to reach the core of whatever subject we try to explore. May I be your guide in seeking to understand the true concepts and the purposeful meaning of "sleep" from their spiritual aspect, our vital source, is like a pillar of our human structure, maintaining and supporting our overall health and well being. Keeping our interior faculty alive in balanced harmony only felt from within in a human being, will bring us closer to the understanding and the purpose of life and why we are born in the first place. For this, we have to dig deeper, and get to know the true make-up of the species that is man, since we do not live from flesh and blood alone, as science has recently acknowledged–, but cant explain, there is something more *"we don't know"*, referring to this statement:

> *"the first gulp from a glass of Natural Science will turn you into an Atheist, but at the bottom of the glass --- GOD is waiting"*, a statement by Werner Heisenberg / Physicist, acknowledging the governing laws by the Divine Will of the Creator/ God, who rules and holds HIS Creation firmly in HIS hands, which confirms the following:

> *"God is the power who activates Natural-law, the power that nobody has yet seen nor grasped, but who's effect everyone can see if he only wants to do so."*
>
> **Abd-ru-shin**

The knowledge elaborated in the following chapters does not derive from my imagination but is based on perfect governing laws, also known as the *"Laws of Nature"*, expressed in all Creation.

This knowledge of creative Laws of the Divine Will, is explained fully in conjunction with Natural-Science: "IN THE LIGHT OF TRUTH" –The Grail-Message by *Abd-ru-shin* (Oskar Ernst Bernhardt, 1875-1941) showing us clarity of the working in Creation and therefore gives answers in a clear and logical way of ***all the fundamental questions of life.***

> *"The source of the highest order/ God the Creator*
>
> *that activates the Natural Laws;*
>
> *the Power that nobody has yet grasped nor seen, but whose* **effects** *every one daily, hourly,*
>
> *indeed in every fraction of a second, must see,*
>
> *intuitively sensed and observed,*
>
> *if only he* **wants** *to do so."*
>
> **Abd-ru-shin**

Dear Reader, thank you in selecting this book ----- a book that opens the door to what shall be an extraordinary journey behind the world of appearances.

This book is not a read, it is a journey into the "**soul and mind**"; and leads you to the deepest realms of human beings origin, the spiritual *world, connecting and, nourishing the human psyche our / Soul through the powerful spirit-energy-radiation felt from within.*

Since childhood, through observation and the ups and downs of life experiences, I have always felt compelled to write this book – I have lived what I wrote *– and therefore share the knowledge that I am privileged to pass on.*

I hope that this excursion with me will help you in your own journey of life -------- choose an undisturbed secluded place, preferable out in Nature – in your garden or lakeside, read carefully, weigh and examine thoughtfully as you learn how to unlock the power from within, the power within your **"sleeping mind"** *and* **"awakened soul"**, *especially during the time of* **"sleep".**

Read on my friends .... and live your Dream.

FOREWORD

My fascination with the radiant world of the Universe, the awe-inspiring cosmos, began in my earliest youth. As far back as I can remember, as a hobby I searched the night-sky for star formations and symbols, and successfully detected their displayed images (acknowledged and documented by science and by the great astronomer Nostradamus) and proudly could identify them by name, like a little girl would remember what her father once told her? That was as far as I could reach into this mysterious Cosmos and felt as if I would have some sort of a personal connection to Nostradamus himself in this silent star communications. Michel Nostradamus, well known as a master astronomer and astrologer, and medical doctor lived on earth 500 years ago, and is still known in every corner of the globe. His fame has not diminished because his accuracy in predicting events based on star constellations continues to fascinate us. My curiosity as to where he drew such knowledge, a knowledge of events hundreds of years forward in time, never left me and can now be answered.

What was considered "mysterious" then can now be explained with the knowledge of the up-building Laws in Creation, laid out in the classic work " In the LIGHT of TRUTH." It is a knowledge that leads to an understanding of the interconnectedness of the invisible energy pulsating through and supporting the visible plane to which our planet earth belongs and we human beings inhabit. The acknowledgment by science of the existence of a *"conscious energy"* is in fact a recognition of spirit radiation, the essence of existence, which is interwoven and runs through the fabric of Creation to underscore all movement. It supports and influences all living forms, including human beings; it strengthens our vital core, which we can experience during our phase of sleep every night.

However, I would not know the nature of the connection I always felt with Nostradamus the famous Astronomer and Seer of the future until that day when, through mysterious circumstances, I inherited his "Egyptian Dream Interpretation Book "the last book in existence/1928. It had been declared "lost" in all archives in Europe, but I was now holding it in my hand and calling it my own. His interpretation of dreams is based only on "intuitive perception", our inner guidance that is also registered during the REM phase of sleep. Therefore it differs from all other dream books available–it speaks for itself.

Destiny was in the making, as I know now!

Dreams or dreaming is a personal inwardly companion throughout life. Do we not especially in times of distress pay greater attention to our nightly visions in the hope of obtaining some clarity and resolution?

Of all the many civilizations that preceded our own, the oldest one of which we are aware that studied the true meaning of dreams were the Egyptians and Syrians. Documentation dating back more than 4000 years are kept in the British Museum in London. Both the Egyptians and Syrians were masters in this providence of cosmic dream-knowledge. Later the Greeks and the Romans continued to build upon the achievement and Nostradamus 450 years ago, with a gift of enlightened communication, was able to bequeath us his refined source of dream knowledge, giving us insight into our tomorrow. His Dream Interpretations are as truthful as his predictions were; history holds the confirmation.

Our intuitively perceived images (dreams) during sleep are only one source of obtaining revealed information about our private life and about our future. **Nostradamus' dream interpretations are of this kind.**

Science has caught up with the famous astronomer and physician and confirmed the deep-seated sources of cosmic radiation, and that sleep and dream are integrated, enabling every human being to tap into the vital energy source that sleep provides and at the same time allowing us a *"sneak peek into our tomorrow."*

Let me acquaint you with an indelible dream experience from my early youth. There was such an unusual and outstanding clarity of images that in that decisive moment I sensed intuitively that *there must be more behind it!* I had to find out –and so I did.

Remembering that frightening situation, seeing myself walking on a cobblestone street in a empty city with only a horse walking right beside me, its big head looking at me, was unnerving. Suddenly the horse took off. How scary it was seeing this big **horse bolt and fall.** *Terrified, I ran off in a different direction trying to escape – and woke up.*

Not long afterwards, I mentioned this unusual dream to an elderly lady friend at my workplace in the hope of getting some answers. To my surprise, she offered me her **Nostradamus Dream Book** to look it up. That was the first time I not only came in contact with the rare book but that I knew of its very existence. To my astonishment, there was under the sub-heading "seeing a horse bolt and fall" this: *"coming into danger of death through carelessness."* Here was the answer; *my dream had a message, namely* **warning me of an impending accident**. It was confirmation of what I suspected; namely two days later, on a Sunday, I was run over by a motorcycle while crossing the street on the way back from church. When I woke up in a hospital bed with head injuries, broken bones and a concussion, I remembered very little how I got there. But I do recall resolving decisively to pay attention to nightly dreams and not ignore their meaningful warnings. On the other hand, they also hint us of good fortunes to come. Science has in the meantime also acknowledged *"the power of stars and planets"* and how they move us humans, confirming this reliable source of powerful communications.

Looking back at history and past civilizations, when the influence of an invisible and reliable cosmic power was taken very seriously, it was common for a monarch to consult court astrologers. seeking advice from the stellar constellations of star aspects what is the same powerful source for visionaries, and can also inform and influence our intuitively perceived dreams. We all can experience it and it can be decisive in making decisions concerning our daily life.

A few of the heads of state who in our time have consulted the star positions in seeking advice before making conclusive decisions affecting their society include:

Francois Mitterand   Boris Jelzin   Ronald Reagan

France   Russia   USA

History has documented positive and decisive leadership in their time in office that was beneficial to their society and the world.

The devastation of Europe in the Second World War many publications pertaining to Nostradamus where lost including his dream book. I tried desperately to buy this book but, unfortunately, it was not available any more in any bookstores.

Many years later, when fate brought me to Canada, I did not give up the hope of one day finding this rare book somewhere. I searched in libraries in Europe, but to no avail. Deeply saddened I was informed by the State Library in Leipzig, Germany, that it had been officially declared *"lost" Das Egyptische Traumdeutungsbuch / The Egyptian Dream Book"*, by Nostradamus. This was my only hope of obtaining a copy.

Some 20 years went by. While on a trip back to my home country Germany, still holding on to the hope of one day finding this rare dream book again, I decided to locate my friend's family in a last attempt to buy her book at any price. Upon my visit, her son informed me that she had passed on. In my disappointment at seeing my mission unfulfilled, my hope dashed, I still asked him if he knew of the existence of his mother's Nostradamus Dream Book!

He looked at me in silence for a moment – as though someone had finally come to claim it. With a proud smile of relief he told me to wait while he retrieved it from the attic. When he handed it to me I heard his words: *"I know that my mother would have given this to you, because she liked you very much and knew how desperately you wanted it for yourself; here, it is yours."* Deeply moved and realizing that I was not "dreaming" but it was reality and finally mine ---- I wondered for a moment *if it was perhaps meant to come into my care?*

Overwhelmed I returned to Canada, clutching my treasure tightly.

For many decades I enjoyed this book immensely. It had its place on my night table and became a steady confidant to inform what lies ahead. I could rely on its guidance and for decades I had the opportunity to test its accuracy. I can proudly testify to its truthfulness today. It gives us the confirmation that the Love and helping Hand from our Creator,/God shown in many ways in His Work of Creation, is guidance available to us if we are willing to open ourselves inwardly in order to "receive". With great precision and economy of words Nostradamus focuses on the essential meaning of the *"symbols seen in a dream."* Elaborate explanations are unnecessary, because what we call a *"true dream", thus perceived intuitively, correspond only with nature's clear universal language of images.*

In 1996 I followed my inspiration unknowingly that was the year of *"acknowledgment"*, according to astronomy, to revive and translate the last remaining copy of the Dream Book from the German edition from 1928 .the only one in existence. This first translated book that I have preserved from extinction for the world was published **on the 500th anniversary year of Nostradamus in 2003, and is now available in 5 languages.** www.nostradamusdreams.com

Nostradamus wrote:

> *"The one who is reasonable can learn from my prophecies how to find the right path to take as if he would have found footprints in the sand from someone who has gone before."*

I feel privileged in revealing in this new extended edition '*Hidden Treasures of Sleep*' this vital source what "sleep" provides us, namely to recharge our inner faculty, our soul, every night with new energy and strength, *which is the actual purpose of why we must sleep.*

By objectively examining the theory as explained in the following chapters leads to a confirmation of its undeniable value and truth.

NATURAL - SCIENCE AND NOSTRADAMUS!

Five centuries ago, Nostradamus, the world's most famous prognosticator astronomer, astrologer and physician, recognized that cosmic forces pervading planets and stars not only determine events here on earth but also influence our human make up organism. Now science has caught up with history's wise man.

Recent scientific research has determined that a *conscious energy radiation* indeed generates movement, holding the universe and planet earth in active balance. Each cosmic body radiates in its own characteristic way. Our established Zodiac Signs validate the influence of the 12 different planetary characteristics. Being born under one of these Signs we show the particular characteristics in our character. Nostradamus knew as a physician about the receptiveness and how our human functioning organism is subject to the influence of cosmic radiation, *touching our innermost core daily and also during our phase of sleep.*

In addition, the physicists Max Planck and Albert Einstein, Nobel laureates in physics in 1918 and 1921 respectively, have confirmed many of Nostradamus' ancient assertions. *Abd-ru-shin* (Oscar Ernst Bernhardt) explains in his unique book of Natural Science - Philosophy "IN THE LIGHT OF TRUTH", the complete uniformity of the governing Cosmic Laws in correspondence with the Spirit-Radiation by the Divine Will of the Creator/God, that is woven into the entire fabric of existence, and man's rightful position in the cosmic rhythm.

Testimonials:

"The actual, the real, the true is not visible transient substance, but the invisible immortal Spirit." Physicist Max Planck

"We must finally learn to distinguish between the spirit and the intellect, the vital core of man and his tool!

"... physical reality is an illusion and only masks a deeper reality where radiation and energy are the form and substance of life."

"For there is life only in radiation, and only in and through radiation is movement generated."

"...there always rests in everything only the same simple Law. In the finest spiritual as in the coarsest earthly. Without changes and without deviation takes effect and must be observed." Abd-ru-shin

"The new world - vision calls upon us to abandon many of our deep-rooted world-views, our firmly-held ideas." Gary Zukav- Physicist USA

(His statement refers not only to natural science but to all aspects of life.)

"The oneness of nature manifests in its laws."
Manfred Eigen, Nobel Prize in Chemistry 1967

"The only source of knowledge is through experience".
Albert Einstein/ Germany 1921

Albert Einstein makes reference to participation of "intuitive perception", thus the involvement of the soul with the core of spirit, in our volition and action. We thereby *"feel' from deep within"* in the experience of dealing with life situations; only then can we actually claim *"to know"*. Our daily family interactions, for an example, provide the best opportunities to *"experience"* life and to attain what we call *"knowing"*. The human soul is our private "receiver station". Its finer antenna registers what we *"feel"* in situations we describe as *"being touched by "*. The experiences we so acquire bear value for who we are, whom we like to become and subsequently shape our personality. They imprint our soul; they are like our personal data that is stored away for us and transcend this world into the beyond, thus inscribing our name in the permanent book of life in accordance with the Cosmic Law of Reciprocal Action: *"What you sow, you will reap."*

The more of such valued imprints we can call our own shape not only our personal identity but also glow through a person's behavior and conduct. *Such a person embodies "human nature" at its best.*

Sadly, however, the **dominance of the intellect rather than the spirit** in our contemporary condition, the outcome of the over-cultivation of the intellect over thousands of years, interferes with and blocks the connection of this finer antenna. This prevents the registration of a *"deep feeling from within"* and a *rightful claim "to know".*

All we claim *"to know"* is largely **borrowed information**, not our own personal experience but that of others. School knowledge or erudition for an example, acquired or learned with our brain activity with no impact on our soul, is the difference to which Einstein alluded:

... Knowledge comes from knowing, and knowing only derives from experiencing felt deep within, when we are "(touched by)" therefore only experiencing can form the bridge from the **subconscious** *to the* **conscious**, *for our Spirit/Soul to mature in the world of matter.*

The invisible immortal Spirit, the eternal light – radiation is the essence of existence generating and sustaining life.

What is destiny? When incorporating this living power of 'divine light' felt from within into our plans and deeds of our everyday life, we automatically shape our destiny in the best way possible, by the self acting governing laws in reciprocal actions.

THE POWER OF THOUGHTS!

Scientific investigations confirm the effective power of what are invisible thoughts. Tests show how thoughts work. Thoughts can be compared to innocuous snowflakes, which build up to unleash the destructive force of an avalanche – small causes therefore can generate great effects. Picture the internet in our age: this meeting place of piled-up "thoughts", such a gigantic breeding ground and the consequences? We must face in accordance with the natural divine law! Hard to imagine, is it not?

What tremendous responsibility lies in this fact for every individual human being?

Every action is preceded by **"thought"**, *and then follows* **word**, *turning into* **deeds**, *which manifest in visible material reality.*

MESSAGE OF WATER

Top: Water from Emoto's hometown, to which 500 people sent good thoughts...

Left: Form created by the influence of "you make me sick". Right: Polluted water

The work of the Japanese investigator, Masaru Emoto, described in his book **"Message of Water"**, reveals consciousness in drops of water. His findings attracted worldwide attention recently and confirm the presence of a **spirit radiation** pulsating through the fabric of exis- tence, as a **"conscious energy"** that science has also acknowledged as already mentioned.

Masaru Emoto's photographs show the most harmonious and beautiful formations of crystals in a drop of water to which good and noble thoughts were directed. In contrast, formations associated with evil thoughts such as: you make me sick, or, I will kill you, show no orderly pattern but merely a confused mess.

This confirms that concentrated thoughts can make something happen.

Similar experiments chime with listening to classical music. Mozart's music, in particular, complete by lawfulness of the tonal structure and therefore in perfection of harmony, moves and activates the human Soul and recent experiments show that therefore boosts the learning ability in schoolchildren. In other words, when Soul and Brain interact in balanced harmony thus the "spiritual and the earthly" faculties of our human condition, in harmonious inter action this assures success in everything we do because the brain is meant to function only as the tool of the Spirit / Soul in command.

In expressing purified thoughts, for example, this we also *call prayer*. In return, when we are showered with blessings, are the answers to our prayers, we can recognize the self acting laws at work (known as reciprocal action, bearing the Will of the Creator – *what you sow you will reap*. It is a confirmation of the power of the Spirit in action in the material world.

Therefore, going to sleep with a cleansed, purified conscience is so vital to connect with higher planes that we enter every night to *recharge our soul,* thus regaining new strength for a new day to begin. It also assures us a better clarity of the images we are able to visualize, which Nostradamus interprets in his "Egyptian Dream Book".

Like plants in nature seeking sunlight that is essential for their growth and development, so can we human beings strive through pure thoughts, good deeds and in noble conduct practice what we understand as virtues in ascent to our Light – the Spirit, glowing and radiating through our own personality on our life's journey.

The *intellect*, our brain the thinking machine activity, is assigned naturally only *as our tool*, as a servant to the Master what is the Spirit in us. converting our volition from the intuitive, creative self, our soul-spirit, into material form. In the intertwined cooperation of spirit, mind and body, we would be in tune with Mother Nature's principles of harmony and goodness and we would earn as a result, according to Natural Law, in reaping what we have sown–also known as Reciprocal Action. *This is the key we hold in our hands, in shaping our own destiny.*

Where harmony is missing, there is no beauty!

We human beings are the highest developed species in the material world, therefore we are not only responsible for our actions with regard to ourselves but we are also responsible for taking proper care of Planet Earth and its other inhabitants. We have the obligation to respect and maintain Nature's principles by its perfect design (Creators-Will) in order to maintain its beauty and orderly rhythm. But instead of following in its path and adjusting to its fundamental mechanism, we disturb and interrupt its divine order. The consequences of man's environmental abuse, for example, are hitting us hard in an unprecedented severity of Nature's unleashed forces, it is the voice from an angry planet. Nature is on a rampage presently; we are helplessly exposed to evident devastation and destruction throughout the world, *including climate change.* Nostradamus warned us long ago.

His prophecies are thought to portend *"doom"*, but they do nothing more than show us *"the visible effect"* of Creation's Law, the consequence of our wrongful actions and behavior over centuries *in repercussion*, the reciprocal action of Nature's self-acting Law of *cause and effect – "what you sow you will reap'*. Therefore we must not only respect these Laws, but also fear and cannot escape their consequences, as already acknowledged 450 years ago!

> We see Nature's Law in full swing," *The Wrath of God sweeps us with an iron broom, as Nostradamus refers to the events at present time manifesting across the entire planet."* We must finally recognize our failure in not living in harmony with Mother Nature, neither in ourselves nor in the relation with our fellow human beings. In disregard, we kill and destroy everywhere we look, with no understanding of our individual and collective contribution to this disasters.
>
> *Small causes, great effects, made visible through Nature's self-acting Laws.*

There is no God who torments men. But there is a kind, merciful God who helps men. He lays upon no one more than he has incurred for himself" ———————————————————————*Buddha.*

In allowing our social and moral development to jump the tracks of the natural order, the misconduct of our so-called "modern age" cannot pass by with impunity according to the divine law. Should we then be surprised by such epidemics of cancer, aids, and corona virus emerging like the scourge of humankind, with no cure in sight, aids epidemic, the social and moral derailment in society, to mention only a few devastating plagues of our present time?

And then we complain when Nature's force unexpectedly hits us seemingly out of the blue. ***Why me? What have I done? I am a good person. It is unfair, and so forth,*** ..... thereby agitating against the Creator's Divine Will, which manifest in His perfect operating Natures Laws to which we have not adapted. Or, when Mother Nature sweeps through unannounced and unpredicted, destroying what we have built up over centuries, we also question its activities as "unfair"? Have we forgotten *Whose Divine Will* is in charge we so depend on? Thus the Will of God the Creator that allows us to be on earth in the first place, passing through as guests, and gave us from the outset an orderly design plan mechanism laid down in Laws to live by? And what about Nature's natural order that is meant to teach us everything we need to grasp for our conscious development? We have cut off our connections to Mother Nature and strayed from the rules we should live by for our own happiness and joy on planet earth. Furthermore, we are not tired of finding all kinds of excuses for the dilemma mankind and the world is in but fail to look at ourselves first for where the cause may lie.

Nature and her laws demand motion in everything and punishes those who disobey the simple laws. God does not punish men as many people imagine. Men punish themselves. Our Creator has no need to interfere, to punish or reward, because His self acting laws are so perfect that they do all the work for Him .It is the Divine-laws which " Judge" man and his activity !

When will we finally give the " honor of perfection " to the source of the highest order—to God /our Creator ?

The priority in restoring " humanity" oriented to our social life, to our broken –down family structure, and also to the political affairs of governments around the world should be foremost aimed and directed at the well being of their own society and their fellow human beings across the globe, instead of selfish political gain and self- proclaimed superiority over others, as we see everywhere. in the world, that would be a big step the only step forward in regaining our fundamental roots of *the lost spiritual nobility*., human beings carry within them . The effort of all people of goodwill on earth is required to get the planet, our home, back and stabilized in its fundamental orderly structure where peace, harmony, joy and beauty fill the air we all like to breath again.

> " *Be the change you wish to see in the world* "!
> Mahatma Gandhi

When will we wake up? --- or is it too late?

SECRETS OF THE UNIVERSE!

It has a beginning but no end...

According to astrophysics, the universe began with the "Big Bang" about 13.5 billion years ago, or should we in contrast say with the ***"Big Command"***, because of the fact that the universe came into being out of a ***Higher Will.*** Has the concept of "blind chance" had its day? It becomes ever more evident to science that there is a very precise design plan for Creation.

The cosmos projects such gigantic powerful forces and galaxies are in constant movement, accelerating farther and farther into boundless expansions and dimensions that a human brain can in its limitation hardly comprehend. Many great minds probe the universe and become humbled and transformed by their experience.

> *"The more we explore of the Cosmos, the less we understand of it."* (Professor Harald Lesch, Astrophysicist, Munich, Germany)

It is not possible nor is it intended for the limited capacity of the human brain, the mere tool of our spirit, of its own accord to reach beyond the earthly domain of time and space. It is no use seeking to understand the whereabouts of celestial bodies, how they came about, or what they are made of if such a quest yields ***no benefit for the maturity of our spirit, which is the actual purpose of our being here on earth.*** We are a complete designed species that is meant to mature toward perfection in this wonderful Creation, provided with all challenges available, which takes us on a temporary pilgrimage of *experiencing life on earth*, as Nostradamus reminds us in one of his quatrains: *"we have everything under our feet to walk on, as we would be in heaven."*

How senseless is it then to wade into space?

Man is not even capable of taking care of his fellow humans here on earth, nor of preserving Mother Nature's environment and keeping it safe, as is essential for all living creatures and should be a priority for us. Instead, we seek to penetrate territories out of reach while ignoring the laws in completeness governing our Planet Earth, our home we are born into, perfect " As It Is ", since the beginning. But mans ego of self proclaimed superiority and arrogance further destroys her perfect designed operation.

Knowledge of the autonomy of the spirit–radiation pervading the cosmos leads us to a further understanding of the fundamentals of our existence and to the actual purpose of life here on earth. Instead of taking this into consideration and willing to live as true human beings who adapt to the natural rhythm of our planets ruling order we try to drive our disintegrating influence into unknown expanses, seeing such as an advantage when in reality it is a great disadvantage. ***Nostradamus*** already warned us 450 years ago of the consequences of irresponsibly intruding into space and acting to interfere in the cosmic ruling order.

He was and is today not wrong in his prognoses concerning the *"radical changes" taking place in the cosmos and here on earth* since the new Millennium in response to the damage done to the benevolent abode bequeathed to us for our development. We witness unexpected disasters around the globe almost as a daily occurrence, Mother Nature's unleashed power is in full force, *like an angry planet in retaliation at the present time and science tries feverishly to find answers to this dilemma.*

We take for granted Mother Nature's benevolent care and provisions, which we should honor. Instead, we abuse her perfect structure and disturb her lawful operation.

The consequences of devastation and the hardship that man must then endure have yet to reach their peak, as foreseen by the astronomer Nostradamus. But man is blind to see and change course before it is too late.

Ancient civilizations considered the heavens to be the dwelling of their deities and the abode of the Creator-God, attaching a high honor and respect to such consideration. The vast universe with billions and billions of stars radiating in the unknown expanse of the firmament has fascinated human beings since time immemorial. Man gazed up to this majestic distant cosmic world shining down on us and resonating a sense of comfort, feeling being "protected" and accepted its benevolence in humility. But that was then, but not so anymore. Have we lost our connection to the above, the divine ruling force, by our Creator/God we so depend on ?

Nostradamus warned: *"The cosmic catastrophes, the revolution taking place in space since the new Millennium began, will increase through the absurdity and interference by man."*

The climatic changes and catastrophes unleashed on earth are the "effect" of the constantly changing planetary configurations, in preparation of the earth's predicted "pole jump" ? is it now in full swing ?

Is our planet facing a radical upheaval? Is another (magnetic) pole shift or a great flood imminent?

The impression is widespread that something is wrong between **"Man and Nature"**, with alarming signs that are becoming unstoppable: *increasing global warming; extreme disorder in climatic changes; distractive floods around the globe, earthquakes reaching #8 on the Richter Scale (10 is the highest with total devastation); unexplainable increase in deadly tornados (over 400 in the US alone recently); glacier meltdown in the north pole; the electric magnetic field in decline.*

Severe catastrophes in Nature has to be seen as unavoidable from the approach of an event of a pole jump (as documented by historical record, and suggestive of the biblical great flood ((Noah)) and the sunken Atlantis Empire thousands of years ago), is a repeating cycle occurring every 7000-8000 years on planet earth ?

Such a gigantic change of a (magnetic) pole shift on planet earth takes place when *"a crisis of humanity"* culminates, it is indeed an undeniable fact at the present time. The real reason was and is, the ushering in of **a *spiritual renewal of mankind*,** when the earth is scheduled to be lifted into a higher orbit of cosmic oscillation according to Divine Ordinance, (by God the Creator) which history has proven and also Nostradamus predicted Turning-point for mankind *"renewal of man, - spiritual awakening"* with the beginning of the New-Millennium.

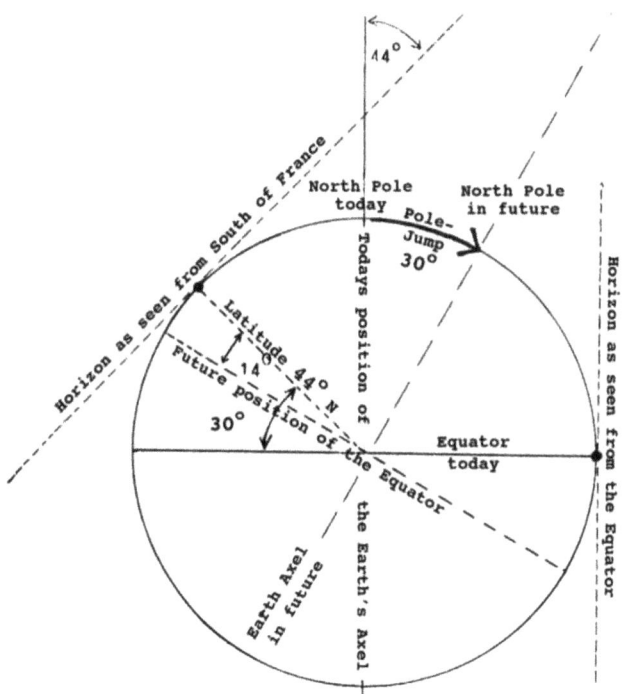

"Every prophecy is imprinted in the book of life...when the Light surrounded me and spoke in the universal language of images, it was not myself but the divine spirit - light communicating through me."
Nostradamus.

He predicted a pole jump by 30 degrees. From the viewpoint of Salon, France, where Nostradamus lived, the globe, our world, would look like this:

Astronomy is the oldest natural science. Over the course of thousands of years it has been acknowledged as our driving force, the so-called engine of human civilization and cultures.

Should we not ask ourselves why we hardly find these days on earth what can be seen as, or be rightfully called a *"civilization in humanity"*, where the noble intensions of the spirit dominates our actions, and serving our fellow man in good deeds is evident what is the foundation of a *"culture"*?

Culture comes from cultivating; cultivating is the result of ennoblement through our spirit, / we know as our soul, felt from within, which is the core of our being and which we must exert to save humankind and also our planet.

What is it then that we deny ourselves in not accepting this ancient knowledge and deep-rooted wisdom? Is it arrogance, ignorance or an ingrained self-acclaimed superiority of man's ego that blocks for example science from accepting the findings of one of its own long ago, when the physicist Max Planck openly acknowledged:

"The actual, the real, the true, is not visible transient substance, but the invisible immortal spirit – in radiation!"

Accepting and incorporating these facts in research would have given science the *"key"* to unlock the true make-up of man as more than flesh and blood. Body, mind and spirit, as three identities independent in origin, should operate in a harmonious unity in the whole human condition. This would, for example, finally enable a root-and-branch treatment of diseases and eliminate recurrence altogether. It could also have distinguished when *"life"* actually begins in an embryo in the womb of an expectant mother, and when life ends at what we understand as *"death."*

Dr. Richard Steinpach further explains this cycle of life in his book: *"Why we live after death? What is the meaning of life?"*

DISCOVER THE SECRETS OF SLEEP

Natural Science – Spiritual Purpose!

SLEEP is one of the most natural and essential aspects of our life. While we may think of sleep as a nether phase of the body at "rest" and in inactivity, it is actually quite an active and busy period of a human being, subconsciously. Therefore we must finally differentiate the *spirit from the mind*–the actual *core of man and his tool.* But let us first look at the scientific conception of "Sleep."

Scientists have studied the physical dimensions of sleep, called polysomnography. It is a diagnostic test to measure and record various physiological variables of the sleeping human body. Sensors are attached to the patient to measure such parameters as brain electrical activity, eye and jaw muscle movement, leg muscle movement, oxygenation levels, airflow, respiratory activity, EEG (electroencephalogram), EKG (electrocardiogram) and the properties of REM-sleep (rapid eye movement).

Science has differentiated the stages we pass through before we enter the last phase of deep sleep (REM-sleep); it is a phase we want to reach as much as possible without disruption .Our nightly journey into sleep can be compared taking a trip into the unknown. But it need not be so with the knowledge of the true make-up of the human being. The fact that we do not exist of flesh and blood alone implies that we must delve into our inner being and get to know the *"soul" (with its core of spirit)* in order to ascertain "what makes us human."

Let us compare for a moment:

Consider: We plan going on a trip don't we all having in mind to look at our best and making sure that we appear neat as possible? Should we not similarly also prepare our inner being to be most purified for a trip into a different sphere, just in case it could be our last physical preparation before entering the unknown, when going to sleep? After all, there is no guarantee that we will return and wake up in the morning. Our conscience therefore should also be cleansed of all accumulated impurities by simply acknowledging our misdeeds, so that the soul is *spotless*, in our most inner beauty and ready to soar. It can then travel carefree and uninterrupted to its plane of origin, which the state of "deep sleep" allows us to reach.

Our two faculties–physical and spiritual–are now prepared for the everyday nightly journey of going somewhere – and in reality we actually do, entering the homogeneous ethereal plane, the home territory of our Soul/ with the core of Spirit.

But first let us clarify the concepts of ***Soul and Spirit***, so as to understand both in their activity leading us to the actual purpose of ***why we need to sleep.***

We have always taken the soul and spirit for granted, talking incessantly about them, ***but what really are they? And where can we find them?***

When we say a person is "high in spirit", this conjures a picture of a well- educated individual, especially one who can articulate ideas brilliantly or displays intellectual wit. But is such a person really high in spirit? Or would it not be more accurate to describe him or her as smart or well educated? Since the human spirit is not materially visible, let me quote the author *Abd-ru-shin* of the work "IN THE LIGHT OF TRUTH – *The Grail Message*":

"Spirit is not wit, and not intellect, nor is it acquired knowledge. It is erroneous, therefore, to call a person "rich in spirit" because he has studied, read and observed much and knows how to converse well about it.

"Spirit is something entirely different. It is an independent consistency, coming from the world of its homogeneous species, which is different from the part to which the earth and thus the physical body belong.

The spiritual world lies higher; it forms the upper and highest part of Creation. Spirit has nothing to do with the earthly intellect, only with the quality that is described as 'deep inner feelings.'

"To be rich in Spirit, therefore, is the same as 'having deep inner feelings' (our inner voice) but not the same as being highly intelligent."

Let me further summarize:

The spirit in us humans is covered or "cloaked" in different consistencies of matter in compliance with Nature's ***"dress-code", and can only be felt by our Soul*** taking on the *"blueprint"* according to Creator's - Gods Will. The spirit needs the cloaks fitting into Mother Natures design in order to be effective in the very dense consistency of the earthly plane. The spirit, our powerful essence and core of being, is the ***igniting spark*** that is radiant from deep within we perceive and know as *"our soul"*. This is the form as perceived through our *"deep inner feelings"*. It is not only the form in which we exist after shedding the physical cloak and enter the otherworldly afterlife or "beyond" but it is also how we are prior to incarnating in the earthly domain.

When we have acknowledged these facts of Truth and make use of them in our daily life, we are holding the *"living key"* to happiness, inner peace, health, success and our overall well-being in our own hands.

What takes place with our Soul during Sleep?

In sleep our eyes are closed our body is in a state of total relaxation. According to research, this state is achieved when lying in a horizontal position. Body and mind are then in the required state of rest; the mind, our thinking "machine", is at a "low energy" level, with the result that the body's radiation declines. Do we not automatically put a blanket on a sleeping person, reckoning that he or she can easily become cold?

These are the signs when the soul loosens its union with the physical body. The mind has shut down in activity (bear in mind that everything stays connected through *"radiation"*) and the soul is then able to drift off towards its plane of homogeneity in the world beyond. Should the soul / spirit sever rather than only loosen its connection with the body, *"death"* results. ***It is for this reason that sleep is called by science the little brother of death.***

As science research has recorded, that after we have passed the first several phases of the sleep process, is like walking through intermittent peaks as resembling hiking up mountains and valleys, or moving on positive and negative pathways. The picture can be likened to a fight between mind activity, which does not want to let go, and the soul awakening to its assigned activity. The intellect has to be shut off, on the one hand to allow its deserved rest of the frontal brain after the daily exertion of the waking state; on the other hand to make room for the small brain (cerebellum), which is responsible for mediating intuition, to become responsive to the soul now surging in activity with less hindrance from the over-cultivated intellect, as happens during the waking state. Then we have entered the phase of *"deep sleep"* or have *"fallen into"*. My use of the word *"fall"* is deliberate, because everyone in their life has felt this sensation at least once when sleeping, as though actually to fall and the body reacts with a jerk, and we wake up suddenly, totally confused but relieved, realizing that the "fall" was only in our dream and not in physical reality, sends us happily back into sleep.

We also can observe on the face, of a sleeping person in what stage they travel at the moment. Eyes closed, no movement, the facial expressions suggesting a certain unreachable distance–you are hesitant not to disturb and snoring may set in. This person is "truly out"; not even a door slamming can wake him or her. It is *"deep sleep",* known as **REM** *-sleep* (rapid eye movement). Studies demonstrate that in this stage of sleep the eyelids are closed but the eyeballs are in constant movement, the eyes looking up as though the individual is climbing or is looking down to pick something up from the floor, suggesting living events taking place and indeed having now arrived in our so-called vivid "***dream world***".

We spend almost a third of our life sleeping, but we are only now beginning to realize that something happens which was unrecognized in its significance for a long time and yet so important for our mental and physical health combined. Considering how much time is involved, could we have imagined sleep as inordinately wasteful? And yet without sleep we could not exist. *"The sleep cycle keeps us humans in balance"* is the premise of an advertising slogan used to sell sleeping pills, which unfortunately have persistent unwanted side effects over time.

Sleep depravation is an alarming trend in our society like never before.

Today millions of people can no longer have an uninterrupted good night's sleep. What can account for the loss of this major resource to nourish the soul and which is vital for our mental and physical health capacity? It was once so natural to tap into, but now seems to have disappeared. The disrupted harmony in the interaction between the small brain (cerebellum) and the frontal brain is mostly to blame because we allow the dominance of the intellect, taking over and being in control, neglecting our spirit (known as inner voice…), in our way of life is mostly to be blamed for the cause of this dilemma; it throws us off balance. This over-cultivation of the intellect is at the expense
of the finer activity of the instrument of our small brain (cerebellum), which serves as *"bridge"* between the subconscious (intuitive) and the conscious (intellectual) mind. Its mediated intuitive communication is interrupted and largely cut off by the interference of the intellect we have over developed since thousands of years creating a "monster.," we follow its dictatorship .

All living creatures, man included, participate in the ever-repeating cycle we call life and are subject to the requirement of sleep in adjusting to the cycle of day time and night time, the entire Nature is under this repeating cycle. During the day our physical activity responds to the sun's energy. However, when the sun sets, making room for the moon to shine and the firmament to light up, we prepare for our nighttime of rest. We also can observe in events in nature the silent transformation, apparent for example when a flower in full bloom during the day literally bows after sunset in a humility of its own and enters its time of rest. Other species close their calyces, the natural sign of going to sleep. This repeating process can be compared to *"changing guards"*.

The day shift comes to an end and the night shift begins for all life forms on planet earth.

We have no choice but to surrender to this natural inviting directive since our day- conscious mind, is also bound to take a rest under this shift change. We are now unconscious of what takes place around us, because our mind is shut off and we have "fallen asleep".

But sleep is not absolutely necessary for the body such as we assume we need when tired. Mere rest can also be sufficient. But we know from experience that rest alone, without such as eight hours of sleep, would not make us *"fit" for the next day.*

If we want to find the source of this breakdown in our sleep capacity we have to step over the physical boundary of our senses into the invisible activity and power of the beyond, where "intuition", an attribute of our core of being our Soul is at work.

The state of deep sleep is the decisive phase when the two faculties, the day- conscious mind on the one hand and the subconscious soul-oriented perception on the other hand, change their respective priority.

Then, when the intuitive channels are cleared for the soul to travel beyond the time and space domain of the earthly and enter a finer eternal sphere belonging to a higher plane in Creation, the soul can than bathe in an atmosphere of snow white purity in order to be refreshed and nourished and thereby gain strength for a new day to begin.

Therefore the energy level that is so crucial for us to begin a new day is not replenished only by resting the body. **We need to sleep in order to "recharge" the soul/spirit our core of being,** and therefore bring about an equilibrium in our overall condition, such as in the balancing of scales.

This is the actual purpose of sleep!

What more evidence do we need that the enduring support to revive us daily issues from a different world than that to which our body belongs?

As soon as we take better care of our inner faculty in order to stay *"connected"*, we will experience our desired good night's sleep with all the values available for us.

… *Relax* (our mind), *refresh* (the way we think), *recharge* (our soul)

In relaxing, simply listen to your echo from within; change your mood; distance yourself from the nagging mind and shut it off. Refresh by observing the beauty of Nature for an example. Let the magic of classical music transform you; you feel as if lifted onto a cloud, like entering a lighter, worry-free zone, which comforts you entirely when your inner senses are open; your heart rejoices, the inner and the outer being are then connected in harmony.

Our soul, a human being's invisible essence, and feeling its evident presence can be confirmed in the next chapters.

"There always rests in everything only the same simple Law, in the spiritual as in the earthly, it takes affect and must be observed."
/ – Abd-ru-shin

To this effect I would like to bring an example in a simple analogy with a car!

Every component of a car is an example of technology engineered in the finest detail in the mind of the inventor, as part of a comprehensive design, with its own place and purpose, and connected to all the other parts in specific and intentional ways. The omission of any one part would cause the whole to be incomplete, so that, quite simply, it could not work. The motor, gas, oil, sparkplugs and any other necessary things could be present, but still the car would not run and would not move.

To get the car started we must first turn on the **switch,** *causing the* **spark plugs to ignite.** *The energy necessary for turning on the motor is thus produced and the car is set for motion.*

Since we are all subject to a uniform Universal Law without exception, let us apply this scheme analogically to the human body.

All living creatures let us remember – and indeed the whole of Creation – exist and function under one uniform Higher Law.

Every organ of our body is masterfully designed according to the Will of our Creator/God, put in place and assigned a specific function; its successful performance of this function is connected to and dependent on the other organs. Just as with the car, leaving out one organ of the body would deprive the whole of the essential characteristic of completeness, and thus interrupt the harmonious cooperation of the whole and ultimately cause it to fail altogether.

The heart *(our engine),* **the blood** *(our fuel) could be in place but still the heart would not be beating and nothing in the body would be moving. To set the bodily mechanism in motion, the* **switch** *has to be turned on;* **igniting the spark in us**, *which is* **the radiating Spirit-germ incarnated in us.** *It is the distribution center for the heavenly radiating fuel, the energy current to activate and set the bodily system in motion, allowing our entire body to move and to function fully.*

Where is the proof, one might ask? Not difficult to find. The answer is *"incarnation of the spirit"* – this decisive moment taking place in the middle of a pregnancy when the first movements of the unborn baby ("quickening") are been *"felt"* by the expectant mother. The spirit, the human core of being, took possession in the prepared physical body in the womb. (remember as I mentioned before –*everything is radiation and only radiation is generating movement, according to Creation laws*) Therefore the blood circulation commences on its own in the fetus together with the heartbeat and a new human life cycle begins, because *the spirit also forms and sustains the blood*. When a human life comes to an end and the spirit leaves the body, the blood has also disappeared, acknowledged by doctors, is what we accept and understand as "death".

If science could overcome the limitations imposed by ignorance or arrogance and would no longer ignore its own findings from long ago by the Nobel laureate the Physicist Max-Planck / 1918, that **radiation of the SPIRIT** is the fundamental source where life comes together, it could confirm today, with no further debates necessary, in which time frame or stage of a pregnancy the actual new life begins, and when it comes naturally to end.

If we fail to maintain the two all-important parts, our physical body and our soul faculty, in harmonious cooperation, neglecting either, our affected engine (our heart), the pumping station, runs out of fuel infusion (the powerful spirit energy). Every engine that runs dry over time is bound to break down. The same will occur in a human body and can therefore shorten life. The affected heart and all the other organs lose the balance of their **natural interaction** and therefore weaken the inner mechanism altogether and affect our overall health. This doomed direction leads to paying attention exclusively to the needs of our physical body only. Failing to nurture the soul/spirit will ultimately cause a major disruption to the natural working order of the body, **leading to stress, discomfort, depression, weakness, illness and even total collapse.**

Keeping the interaction of soul and body harmonious, for example in an overall healthy and happy condition, does not allow any *"depression"* to take hold. ***Depression is not an illness and cannot be silenced with drugs. It is a self-inflicted condition, you allowed yourself slide into;-----you can get yourself out again in activating your inner channels and connect with your God the Creator, in prayer, convinced in your believe in his powerful heavenly healing material for the Spirit/Soul in you, to be granted..!*** . The natural recipe with all its healing ingredients are provided. Take your willpower, free your mind from all worries that try to occupy and bombard you constantly like holding you hostage. Mobilize your deepest feelings. Let your soul speak in sending her sincere longing for help upwards towards heaven and depression will leave you finding its back door out. Fill the gap of emptiness and ***look upwards to the eternal Light –God/ the Creator, connect inwardly with your powerful spirit/ soul, when your believe became conviction, after having understood his governing Laws in Creation and lived by and the "heavenly fuel from above" streaming down on you regaining self-confidence, and depression on your doorstep find no entrance anymore to take over.*** Be receptive ***and believe*** in the powerful heavenly divine flow of light energy, the healing power streaming down on us, from the divine in so many ways, hanging like threads above and around us, always there for everyone to make a connection, of the heavenly nutrition to heal open wounds. Therefore be open inwardly, convinced in your believe of an existing God/our Creator (is like a prayer) and your Soul will receive the *"heavenly fuel of healing nourishment"*, bestowed by the Grace and Love of our Creator /God on all His creatures, and depression will fly off like airborne.

"Give Light and the people will find their own way!"

Every illness has its roots in the mental condition!

The Western World is adapting more and more to an ancient Chinese practice and wisdom that correlates an affected organ with the mental condition in a patient. The documented findings, to mention here only two:

A kidney dysfunction has its roots in ***being fearful***.

A lung tumor in a non-smoker is rooted in suffering from ***constant grief***.

Could this be the cause of an alarming incidence of lung cancer in non-smokers? which is marching to the forefront of killer one, affecting so many young people? I myself recently lost my younger sister to this devastating scourge. When I mentioned the Chinese findings at her deathbed and why she had to die from such an illness, so young and having never smoked in her life, she confessed to having *"**grieved for decades** "*over her broken marriage and family torn apart. The constant inner sadness nagging at our soul weakened over time the healthy cells, of missing the feeding nourishment of your peaceful Soul radiating (causing a creeping onset of cancer); this ***affected her lung and caused it to "break down"***.

How many broken homes and families suffer in our time, caused by sadness and grief? Could this be the basis of the surge in lung decease among non-smokers, and which still eludes science unless it manages to step beyond the physical boundary and accept the findings from its ranks long ago that the human core of spirit is starving due to being undernourished?

For example, when a terminally ill patient is discharged from hospital care and the doctors admit there is nothing more they can do, and yet, in disbelief, they have to acknowledge that *"there is something we don't know"* when a patient cured them self's? Could the answer lie in the fact that our deepest core, our spirit/soul, dispense healing power? It is the same source which nurtures also our immune system and keeps it strong **our natural inbuilt "defense mechanism"** according to Natural Law, that fights off unwanted intruders such as bacteria, virus and other pathogens, attacking healthy cells. Bear in mind: we alone carry responsibility for our own mental and physical well-being in the natural way provided for us.

What more evidence do we need of ours, seeing, that our carried lively vital support, which is obviously from a different world, as to which our body belongs, bear the power of healing.

We can now also clarify the origin of *emotions:* when we experience emotions wrongfully characterized as a *"weakness"* and we even apologize, almost in shame, for getting emotional, such as in shedding tears, for an example. In reality, it is an indication that our inner being is still alive and in harmony functioned a sign that we are capable of *"being touched from within"*, human beings true identity still in tact, means our Soul feels and is alive and we should, for example, be proud of *tears*, its visible expression when unexpected disaster strikes, or a sudden loss touches us deeply, when overwhelming joy evokes inexplicable tears, or hearty laughter brings on tears. Such are enriching values, and a proud sign of *" being still together as a true human-being."*

Emotions are the communicating voice of our soul/with the core of spirit – connecting you with God. "God is Life"

Try as we may, we cannot intellectually command ourselves to be emotional, because emotions originate through intuitive perception and can only be *"felt deep from within"*. The signals released through the appropriate channels pass immediately to the brain (our tool) and become expressed in visible reaction in tears, goose bumps or an involuntary trembling of the body.

In contrast, pain from a physical injury the reaction is reversed. The causing physical pain signals come first, directly from the mind, and tears set in *secondarily.*

Also with *"first impressions"*, the perception, for example, on meeting a person for the first time, the latter's radiating *"aura"* imparts an immediate sense of like or dislike, warmth or caution. This spontaneous evaluation is uncannily on the mark and is never wrong, because the person's core of being is what is been *"felt"*. But should we in the process become more receptive to our rational mind and let our wishful opinions interfere, our evaluation would in the end mostly prove wrong. Listening more to our *"inner voice"* and acting on its pure infusion would always align us on the side of right. Try it, and you will find the confirmation.

The foregoing explanation of the visible and invisible power linking us day and night leads to the actual purpose of *"why we need sleep"*. It was necessary for an overall understanding of the natural rhythm also embracing us humans, so that as we may re- exert the buried activity of our soul., during the time of sleep, without our mind interference.

Hermann Hesse, the German author and poet, Nobel laureate in literature, 1946 summarizes our *"nightly preparation for sleep"* in his poem:

DISCOVER THE HIDDEN TREASURES OF SLEEP!

"Every Evening"

Every evening hold account of your day; was it a joyful one in deeds and loyalty? Or one discouraged in fear and repentance?
Bring to mind the names of your loved ones.
Hate and injustice silently acknowledge from within.
Be deeply ashamed of all wrongdoing, no shadows take with you when going to sleep. Eliminate all worries from your soul, so that it can in far distance in purity might rest.
Then ... in that purified inside of yours you should remember the most precious...
... your mother... your childhood time... ...
See, only then you are pure and prepared to drink from the refreshing fountain sleep provides, where the "golden dreams" appear in consolations, so that you can begin your next day ---
as a **Hero in Victory.**

When I was 10 years old I had to learn this poem by Hermann Hesse in school. It was my favorite as I remember. It must have touched me so deeply that it remained indelibly "engraved" in my Soul, hardly knowing that one day I would take on the subject of *"sleep and dream"* and be destined to preserve from oblivion the only remaining copy of the *"Dream Book" by Nostradamus*, in which the dominance of the soul is evident.

Perhaps we are now in a position to answer the question: **why do millions of people in our time have such difficulty finding refuge in a good night's sleep?** We have lost the connection to our core of being, the soul in us to activate and incorporate in our daily living life. We live to shallow on the surface; our dictating intellectual mind controlling us and we are preoccupied with meeting the pressing demands of technology in supposedly making our lives easier. But the opposite is the case; valuable personal time is in rapid decline, our spirit/soul is sidelined and human values have disappeared.

The priorities we must change when approaching nighttime at least. Every one can *"feel"* a difference at daybreak after a good night's sleep; it feels like being *"together"* again, wrapped in a great deal of self-worth, carrying joyfully a personal responsibility, feels predictive like being a useful member in the large family of humankind, ready to be called to duty, whatever that might be; refreshed and strengthened, we than can take on joyful a new day and be of service.

With this awareness, realizing that the most precious gift, our spirit/ soul the core of life, has been ignored for too long, forgotten and its care neglected, we must bring it to the forefront again in our life in order to remove from the future the destructive consequences we now experience and witness in all aspects and structures of life and on our planet Earth.

As soon as we wake up in the morning, body and soul again restore their firm union. All who enjoy a good night's sleep experience tremendous energy, which provides a joyful confidence to take on whatever comes our way, where fear and weakness have no place. In contrast, those who struggle and have missed a good sleep feel weak with no energy or ambition to take on a new day. There is much truth in the saying, with reference to such people: ***"He is not quite himself"***, or, ***"she is not together!"*** Such a person's scale is just not balanced. Every human soul is able to benefit by drawing from the "highest energy source" that sleep facilitates, or, on the other hand, ignoring it altogether with the attendant consequences we must accept and face.

How many in the present time, mostly through willful ignorance, fail to recognize the ***importance and vital purpose of sleep?***

WHAT ARE DREAMS?

Fantasies or predictive messages?

Dreams accompany us throughout the journey of life. They are part of a communication by intuitive perception, which immediately impresses a picture on the small brain (cerebellum), assigned as a bridge in forwarding information by intuition from the subconscious to the conscious mind. This communication from our subconscious faculty is expressed and corresponds only in *"Natures Universal Language of Images"* that we are able to visualize during sleep and can be called a *"true dream"*.

We spend almost a third of our life in a state of sleep, drifting off into a different world and yet we pay hardly any attention to this important aspect of our life. In fact, it is a great sadness that in our mate- rialistic oriented present time its true meaning and beneficial value have become eroded and are almost completely ignored and forgotten.

Since we now have the knowledge to distinguish the *self* from the ***brain*** as two different identities of a human being, stemming from two different origins, we are able to arrive at the origin of ***true dreams.*** Nature's silent language of living symbols speaks to us what lies ahead. Nostradamus' dream interpretations, as verifiable as his predictions, are a testament to the fact, also confirmed by science, that the invisible planes uphold by radiation the visible sphere, to which our Earth belongs.

The dream phenomenon, as explained by ancient civilizations dating back 4,000 years, is now brought to the surface.

From here on I will apply the terms ***"produced"*** to what originates from our intellect (frontal brain, cerebrum) and ***"perceived"*** to what arises through our subconscious faculty (small brain, cerebellum). This recognition will clarify the category of a true dream and assign it to its correct origin. We have now opened the door through which we can step naturally into the unknown eternal world beyond, which we can enter every night during sleep.

When we start to think our mind is "producing". Brain activity controls our action. We produce thoughts and set in motion what leads to visible deeds. The mind also intents creating fantasies, such as in building castles in the air, and the sky is the limit. How dull would life be without such daydreams, which we fashion in many colors and shapes in our joyous fantasies? Daydreams are of importance especially in youth, when we are filled with a seemingly unstoppable yearning to conquer the world, yet with no awareness where it might lead! Having imaginative daydreams is like holding on to hope, for better things and times might come.

So we keep on dreaming ... and dreaming ...

The founder of psychoanalysis, Dr. Sigmund Freud, is well known for his study of dreams that was published hundred years ago. However, recent media reports have presented his ideas on this subject as being less than reliable. Dream researchers have turned away from Freud's theory because his approach tended to see the explanation of dreams in the psychological condition of the individual, and has provided an enormous and fertile territory for psychiatrists and psychotherapists. Furthermore, researchers have sought to examine the confused imagery with added talking and stories of which dreams consist and that so often leave the dreamer in a state of fear or discomfort creating the so- called 'sleep disorder'.

Some recent scientific reviews have questioned, discredited and rejected Freud's ideas. Years ago, after a convention of dream researchers from around the world, the Sigmund Freud Institute in Germany published a statement to the effect that his analyses ascribe dreams to **nothing more than a worrisome product of the thoughts** we take with us when we go to sleep. In other words, they are only *confused stories that we spit out after digesting the events we were involved in during the daytime.* Waking in the morning, often in fear and perspiration, is nothing else but a leftover, a kind of *"indigestion"* of the mind .

The term "analysis"–the intellectual "tool" of science–describes the method of approach of Sigmund Freud to "produced dreams" in explaining how the mind works. Those who have adapted Freud's theory must be disappointed. Therefore, it is advisable to bear in mind that not everything we see in our sleep deserves the name **Dream.**

We receive *a true dream* by *intuitive perception only;* the waking mind is not involved. This distinction between *"perceived"* and *"produced"* is fundamental. It provides a clear definition of the activities of the *self (spirit)* in us and of the *intellect* operating as *its tool.*

The oldest civilization that studied the meaning of symbols seen in a dream were the Egyptian and Syrians. Documentation dating back 4,000 years are kept in the British Museum in London. Both the high cultured Egyptians and the Assyrians were masters in dream interpretations. Then 450 years ago, Nostradamus substantially expanded this dream knowledge through his high degree of astronomy and as a physician. He acknowledged the interplay of planet and star radiation with our physical body, touching also our soul inwardly in our phase of sleep.

It provides a glimpse into what lies ahead and can shape our daily life immensely. Ignoring silent indications of the symbols and following intellectually dictated decisions only can lead to unnecessary self-imposed problems, as well as make us miss out on joyous events and good fortune that will brighten up our days. I myself have experienced over more than 40 years through the premonitions of dreams that the power of the stars indeed moves us humans.

Nature's images have been recognized for thousands of years as the universal language of correspondence between the invisible plane and our world of matter. It is for this reason that true dreams can only be perceived during nocturnal sleep. They derive from higher planes in Creation and can only be apprehended in the language of nature's living symbols speaking to us.

Nostradamus understood the pulse of the fundamental laws operating uniformly throughout the Cosmos. Only by adjusting to this natural order can we further enrich our personality in achieving a *better physical, mental and spiritual happiness.*

You may have found books that purport to be about dreams in which the author would have you believe that the idea that dreams contain meaningful symbols is nothing more than *ancient superstition* that we in our modern era should have outgrown. Or, on the other hand, that symbols change with society. If the latter is the case, how is it that living symbols such as those of the ever-present trees or flowers never change? Has the rose, the queen of flowers, changed its exquisite design to suit the time? It is a law that

Mother Nature speaks to us in her manifest language, the living and visible form in which she presents herself and which we must respect and honor and also learn to understand. No doubt, if man knew how to change the heartbeat of the structure he would have done so long ago. The very solid nature's imprint speaks to us through its living images in its entire beauty that we enjoy in our lifetime, and thank heaven it cannot be changed by anyone, because it outlives us through space and time.

The Laws of Nature bear the Will of our Creator/God: his manifestation of the spirit pulsing through everything that exists.

Now you may ask: what guarantee do I have of entering the desired dream world?

Sleep provides us the natural resource to travel without a designed plan. Stepping down from the false pedestal usurped by the "intellect" before nighttime and making room for a gentle approach in humility towards a " higher divine Superiority" we actually depend on, is the first step. Distance yourself from the restless nagging mind, which seems to follow us everywhere. We can't allow it, especially not in the evening. We have to leave the package of unresolved matters for the next day to deal with. Leave all business headaches behind when you close the office door and call it quits for the day. Your mind will thank you for unburdening it at least for the evening hours. Put the brain *the thinking machine to rest*.

Create an atmosphere by engaging in personal creativities, where your soul and "feelings" dominate. Dwell for a while in "gratitude", which will set free your inner self. Find refuge in playing an instrument, for example. Music seems to wipe out worries, or simply start to sing, which immediately uplifts you and all the problems and worries fly off like airborne on wings. Drench yourself in ***Mozart music, which is heavenly nutrition feeding hungry souls***; it opens the channels that will ascent you on a carefree journey upwards during the time of sleep.

As soon as we reach the stage of "deep sleep" the soul is able to drift off into the world beyond towards its eternal realm of origin.

It is as if the invisible hand of Mother Nature, escorted by an radiating cosmos takes you by the hand in your subconscious state and guides you to her eventful wonderful world beyond. She opens for you one of her windows to let you see where the universal language of her images is silently being spoken.

Open yourself from within to her gesture of goodness and peaceful guidance in receiving her "warnings" or as she lets you see the good fortune awaiting you in the future. Like every good mother would take her child by the hand in protection when facing danger, or make you aware of the goodness in your heart, you should practice and be thankful to the heavenly provider (God-the Creator) from above.

As soon as our soul has arrived in its plane of homogeneity she than can bathe in the refreshing fountain of youth and beauty. As a bonus gift we are allowed to bring back information concerning our life here on earth when the soul speaks in images. This information should support and reassure us as being on the right track in our immediate plans and help us in everyday decisions we have to make.. It can confirm that joyful times lie ahead, or warn us of difficult times. If we know what is imminent, we can prepare ahead of time and manage situations for a better outcome.

We still have a choice. We can take the advice given through our dreams seriously and act accordingly, or ignore it completely, which, however, does not spare us the consequences we must deal with one day, according to the manifested lawfulness.

In this regard, I would like to share with you a recent incident that happened in my own family.

Around noon on a Sunday at the end of November I returned home from a brief outing to find my husband leaning over the kitchen table with his head down, as if accepting some kind of defeat. I had never seen him in such a condition.

"What is wrong with you?" I asked. "I don't feel well," he said.

I saw that his face was pale, indicating there was something wrong. "You look awful!"

"I am in severe pain," he replied. Then he gasped for air. "Where does it hurt?"

He pointed to his stomach. Oh well, I thought, he must have eaten something that disagreed with him and got food poisoning, or perhaps he was simply constipated.

After he replied negatively to all of my common sense questions, I suggested that he let me take him to the hospital. "No," he said, "I'll wait for a while, it should get better," confirming in my mind his stubbornness, always thinking he knows best.

"Come on, let's go," I urged him, "I can drive you to the emergency room, they are open on Sunday."

"No" he insisted, "I am just going to lie down for a while."

So be it then, I thought, and went upstairs to make his bed. As I ascended the stairs I suddenly remembered those images seen in my sleep three days before in which an old house was burning. The interpretation in the "Dream Book": **"unexpected death, losing your lover."** *I had forced* myself not to think about it then; who wants to dwell on such things when everyone around you is in good health?

Immediately I sensed a connection with my husband's condition, turned on my heels and rushed back downstairs.

"Quick, we are going to the hospital. Now!" "No," he complained, "I don't want to go."

Well, it was time to take charge. I screamed at him "Hurry up! Quick! It could be your heart!" That's what I guessed it was.

Finally I got him into the car and we sped off. "Slow down," he said, "I am getting dizzy ..."

Oh no, I thought, if I don't make it in time ... He moved his fingers. "Are they getting numb?" I asked.

"Yes."

Then I knew it was indeed a serious situation, related to his heart. I stepped on the gas pedal. God help me, I thought, I must reach the hospital, what if he collapses on me now?

We arrived at the emergency ward. There wasn't a wheelchair in sight, he could hardly remain on his feet, and there was no one at the reception desk. I remember hitting a little bell on the counter and saw a nurse approaching us saying to fill in the forms.

"Fill in the forms?" I repeated incredulously. "Get moving, woman! This man is having a heart attack! Move, move." I screamed!

She ran off and returned with a wheelchair, and wheeled him to the area behind the curtains.

Ten minutes later they called me in. I was in a chair not far from his bedside. The actions of three doctors and two nurses around him and the sight of him connected to the monitoring equipment gave me the impression of a situation of extreme urgency.

And how right it turned out to be. One of the doctors approached me and looked at me in silence for a while, perhaps in disbelief that I had not called an ambulance, I thought for a moment!

"Is it over?" I asked. "Is he through his crisis?"

"Oh no," he replied. "It just hit. It's a severe heart attack. We must thank you so much for bringing him in at the right time. Minutes later it would have been too late. He wouldn't have made it."

It's not me you have to thank, I thought to myself, my emotions catching up with me as I silently sent my deepest gratitude up to the Heavenly divine Father.

I was fully aware that by my decision to act quickly I had invoked destiny, and that the action had been prompted by the warning received in my dream days before. In such communication between the invisible eternal world and this world of matter, we can recognize the Love of God for us humans, reading His language in Nature's nightly communication, coming from a different world to guide us in the right direction. This all-embracing love, which warns before facing the unexpected, or when we are being foretold of good fortune, is a tremendous support in our life.

After three weeks in the hospital and a successful triple bypass operation, my husband was discharged home two days before the holiday season and the whole family was united in giving "thanks" in the Christmas -Season of Gods love.

Poets and philosophers have often paid homage to our soul, drawing from those promising fountains of strength in the realm we enter every night, where "golden dreams" smile and wait for us in comfort.

Our nightly journey into the eventful world of the beyond, with our intuitive faculty prepared, is essential for our overall well-being and a major factor preventing us from sleep disorders. It strengthens the union between body and soul, maintaining our inner harmony to stay balanced, so that we can start nourished and refreshed the next day. **That is the actual purpose of sleep!**

Meaningful and valuable dreams can be recognized by the distinctness and clarity the images convey, without spoken words. Bear in mind that in order to speak, the mind must be awake, but it is ordinarily completely turned off in sleep. I suggest that in the beginning, until you have more practice in the slow return from sleep to the waking state, you keep a notebook and pen on your night table. As soon as we intend to wake up, carrying a load of information with us, concentrate and hold on to the images that we saw so vividly only moments before. Write down what caught your most attention. It is very important to try to remain in this half-sleep, half-awake state to facilitate recall of what you have just experienced. Avoid being overwhelmed by the thought that tries to crowd of the freshly brewed coffee should allow your mind suddenly to take over, but it mostly does. Any interruption during the process of transition, when travelling from the subconscious world to the world of waking reality, can be damaging. As soon as our mind takes over, preoccupied with earthly matters, it is very difficult to recall images, because the waking state dominates the mind and overpowers the dream experience. A valuable message can thus be erased. Take your time; do not focus too quickly on your priorities for the day.

Once you learn to interpret your dreams the way Nostradamus did, you will never again face the future-- --unaware,----uninformed---- or afraid!

I will close this chapter with a poem by the Russian author, Alexander Solzhenitsyn, the 1970 Nobel laureate in literature:

THE MORNING!

What really takes place with our SOUL in the nighttime?
From the stagnant silence of sleep, she even gained --- loosened from
the body --- having the ability to travel through luminous, sublime
areas, where she frees herself from unimportant things from past days
or years accumulated, trying still to hold on in its deforming way.

And then ... she is drifting back in its region and state of snow-
white purity, where she is transformed in a state of tranquility.

What are we thinking in those minutes? It seems that suddenly
with all transparency you have understood something that you
never before understood ... that suddenly ... you freeze ... as
though, just in that particular moment, something starts to grow,
from deep within, something you never realized or felt before
and so totally unexpected. Almost without breathing you tend
this bright sprout, the bud of a little white lily, in this moment
growing from a maiden silence of the waters of eternity...

*How comforting are these moments! You literally look down
from above onto yourself. You discover in comparable, deciding to
simply allow your imagination to take off.........hoping.........
that this picture should never lose its clarity, hoping that
nothing should destroy the smoothness of the sea in you.*

*But soon enough, something will squeeze in between and will
destroy the magic of this atmosphere: it could be a disturbance
from the outside, or a word, sometimes a sudden thought, and the
wonder has disappeared. It is not there anymore, the unbelievable,
untouchable, it is not there anymore, the little sea in you, ...
and the whole day you could search and every other, morning',
in bringing back this 'magic state in you,'...... but in vain.*

A statement from a well-known German Philosopher, C.G. Lichtenberg:

> *"It is a privilege of every human being to know
> that we dream and have the 'knowledge'.
> The dream is part of 'life' and should be included
> in our daily life in order to become 'ONE'.
> Only that we should call "**THE REAL LIFE.**"*

I conclude my writings with a quote by the German philosopher and poet J.W. von Goethe 1749-1832,

> "Escape! ...
> upwards ... into a far distant land, and this
> mysterious dream – knowledge from
> Nostradamus' own hand,
> is it not guidance enough for you?"

Nostradamus 1503-1566

NOSTRADAMUS' DREAM SYMBOLOGY FROM A-Z

Nature's Language Speaks

A

Abbess, to see a female abbot: *haughtiness and arrogance. are detrimental to your character.*
Abbot, to see one in his robes: *means annoyance.*
Abundance, to experience: *holding onto false hopes.*
Abduction, yourself, or witness: *unexpected, imminent marriage.*
Accident: *relief from worries.*
Accusation, or accused by others: *restlessness and discontent.*
Accusing others: *troubled success.*
Acorns, gather: *means profit.*
Acorn, or a wreath of acorn leaves: *distinction and honor.*
Acquainted, getting to know someone: *a loss or affliction.*
Adder, seeing this snake: *unpleasant / dangerous acquaintance.*
Adultery committing: *horrendous disagreements.*
Adultery, withstanding a temptation: *triumph over your enemies.*
Advertisement, seeing the ad: *you will fall into disgrace.*
Advertisement or public notification: *work without success.*
Advice, giving to others: *luck in completing difficult business matters.*
Advice, receiving: *you will be deceived.*
Air balloon, to see one fly: *a separation ahead.*
Alcoholic, being one yourself: *happiness and health.*
Almonds, eating: *your nosiness will embarrass you.*
Aloe, seeing this plant: *renewing an old friendship.*
Altar, to see one: *comfort and enjoyment.*
Amber, seeing in a necklace: *receiving a gift.*
Ambush, falling into a trap: *hardship in business.*
Amusement park: *you will be well and enjoy advantages.*
Anchor, to see one: *confirmation of your hopes.*
Anchor, throwing: *great danger ahead.*
Anchovy, eating or seeing: *consistent, good luck.*
Angel, seeing: *lots of luck, confirmation of all hopes and wishes, - welcome news.*
Angel, to become one: *great honor;* **for a sick person:** *means death.*
Angry, being: *irreconcilable enemies.*
Animals, your own, or feeding: *happiness and wealth.*

Animals, various breeds: *associations with unknown people.*
Animals being tamed: *overcoming obstacles, patiently.*
Animals jumping: *loss of freedom or independence.*
Antler, to see these: *disloyalty and treason.*
Ants, seeing: *lots of work, great honor.*
Anthill, hive, stepping into: *you find yourself in bad company.*
Anvil, seeing: *a steady job and secure income.*
Apostle, seeing or speak to one: *receiving good news.*
Apples, exquisite, see or eating: *joy, pleasure, long life, good fortune in love, steadfastness, luck in business and all undertakings.*
Apples, beautiful, cutting: *separation from boy- or girlfriend.*
Apples, sour, eating: *disputes, arguments, sadness, or false friends.*
Apples, many on a tree: *you will get many relatives.*
Apple juice, or apple wine drinking: *efforts in vain, arguments - indecency.*
Apricots seeing or eating: *a late marriage in life.*
April Fool's Day: *experience honor in the near future.*
Apron, putting on a nice one: *receiving presents.*
Apron, made of silk: *fortunate money circumstances.*
Arbor, being under one: *a pleasant acquaintance.*
Archery, to <u>span</u> and shoot: *comfort in your sorrow.*
Archbishop, seeing: *abrupt death.*
Architect, seeing on a building site: *forthcoming danger.*
Architect, giving instructions: *confirms a well-managed life.*
Argument, occurring between friends: *declining prosperity.*
Argument, and winning: *with great effort, improving your status.*
Arguments, with your loved one: *an advantageous marriage.*
Ark, seeing one: *you will become annoyed.*
Arm, being broken: *disaster or death.*
Arm, seeing hairy: *a huge fortune.*
Arm, being wounded: *indicates sadness.* **Arm, having a huge one:** *hard work ahead.* **Arm, having a small one**: *slipping into poverty.*
Arm - bandage, to put one on or several: *sick-bed*
Arm-weapon, seeing many: *conditions will worsen; great unhappiness*
Arm- weapon, been broken: *a dispute will occur.*

Arm -weapon, to see your own: *happiness and honor.*
Arm -weapon being made: *bad times ahead.*
Armchair, seeing: *a comfortable, cheerful life.*
Armour, wearing: *stay away from your enemies.*
Army, to see one in combat: *misery and grief.*
Army, to see marching: *mischief and harm approaching.*
Arrested, being yourself: *obstacles in ventures, fraud and slander.*
Arrow, to see one: *forthcoming hardship, disagreements.*
Arrow, shooting: *you will steer yourself into bad luck.*
Arsenal seeing one: *war times approaching, unrest.*
Artichoke, seeing or eating: *secretly suffering, imminent separation*
Ashes, seeing: *a bitter deception or insult.*
Asparagus, eating or seeing: *good ventures, enjoying trust*
Asparagus, harvesting: *cheerful days*
Asparagus field, seeing: *receiving huge profit.*
Assets: *forthcoming losses.*
Audience, with a dignitary: *happiness and gain.*
Authority, or a person of authority: *bad luck and a lengthy lawsuit.*
Avalanche, to witness one: *affliction and grief.*
Awaken, exceptionally early: *happiness and forthcoming wealth.*
Axe, to see one: *a rebellion, revolt, bad luck in general.*
Axe, to split wood: *means a separation, being apart.*

B

Bacon (ham, smoked meat), eating or seeing: *death of a friend or relative, pursuit by enemies.*
Badger, catching: *loosing your living quarters.*
Bagpipe, playing or hearing: *joyfulness.*
Bag (paper), seeing many: *unfaithfulness.*
Bailiff, seeing or talking to: *warning about bad people, difficulties keeping the first lover; being tricked in business matters.*
Baked goods, eating: *forthcoming harm or troubles.*
Baker or bakery, seeing: *a blessed year.*
Baking bread: *enjoying good nutritious food.*

Baking cookies: *becoming useful to others.*
Bake - trough (kneading) empty: *misery will come your way.*
Bake - trough (kneading) full, seeing: *means great wealth.*
Baker's oven: *good fortune.*
Bald, being: *you are reaching old age.*
Bald-headed person, seeing: *derision, scorn.*
Ball playing: *good prospect into the future.*
Ball, hitting: *disagreements, will continue.*
Ball (a dance), attending: *extraordinary good luck, great honor.*
Ballet, seeing: *deception and cheating.*
Balloon, seeing: *misfortune lies ahead.*
Balcony, standing on: *returned love.*
Balsam, having: *earning praise.*
Bandit, seeing: *means persecution.*
Bang, noise, explosion: *an ill–fated message.*
Banishing someone: *bad luck ahead.*
Bank building: *a flourishing business, secure ventures.*
Banker, seeing: *involvement in gossips.*
Barefooted running: *body weakness, or misfortune.*
Barley, eating: *good health.*
Barley, seeing: *food shortage and worries.*
Barn, seeing empty: *disappointment in your hopes.*
Barn, a full one: *sudden, unexpected wealth.*
Barracks, seeing: *assurance in behavior.*
Barrel, seeing: *beware of gluttony.*
Barrier-gate, breaking: *returning from abroad.*
Basin, in brass or copper: *faithfulness, loyalty.*
Basin, washing yourself: *cleanliness is the essence of health.*
Basket, seeing empty: *indicating losses of all kinds.*
Basket, a closed one: *keeping secrets.*
Basket (with handle) carrying: *worries about the future.*
Basket with flowers: *luck in love.*
Bat, catching: *for ill persons, a quick recovery*
Bats, seeing: *doubtful business success; fickle surrounding.*
Bathing, and not perspiring: *interruptions in business.*
Bathtub water, muddy: *danger of fire.*

Bathing, in clear water: *happiness, health, luck and success in love.*
Bathing, in muddy water: *sorrow, ill-health and bad luck.*
Bathing, in warm water: for an ill person - *health*; **for a healthy person** - *obstacles in business.*
Bathing, in general: *indicates anger.*
Bathing, in the room: *grief, sorrow.*
Battle (a fight, attending): *means seduction.*
Bay-leaf tree: *success in all your projects.*
Bay leaves, picking: *seeing hopes fading away.*
Bay-leaf wreath: *coming into honor.*
Beans, eating or seeing: *dispute, experience misfortune and defamation of character.*
Beans, in full bloom: *a wish will come true.*
Beans, growing: *a purpose is acknowledged.*
Beans, letting them burn: *lot of annoyance.*
Beans, peeling: *worries about the future.*
Beans, planting: *a new business takeover.*
Bears, seeing: *suffering from injustice, bad gossip; furthermore, dreams with hyenas, tigers and wild beasts mean misfortune, quarrels, discord.*
Beard, black, good looking: *means health.*
Beard, grey seeing: *resentment, melancholy.*
Beard, a long one: *profit, gain and luck.*
Beard, in red seeing: *having false friends.*
Beard, seeing on a woman: *annoyance, unpleasantness.*
Beard, shaving off: *losses of all kinds, multiple misfortunes.*
Beast, predacious animal: *beware of deceitful behavior.*
Beast, being beaten or attacked: *quarrel occurring around you.*
Bed, a beautiful one: *happiness, harmony in your marriage.*
Bed, not clean; uncomfortable: *you are unsociable, incompatible.*
Bed, of feathers, shaking, in the sun: *family welfare.*
Bed, seeing burn: *means disaster, illness, death.*
Beds, rain falling onto: *excessiveness.*
Bed, and warm bottle seeing: *soon to be married.*
Bees, seeing: *always a good omen.*
Bees, swarming: *confusing matters, complications.*

Bees, being stung: *imminent bad luck, disagreements with friends.*
Bees, seeing very busy: *living well, --- getting on.*
Bee honey, gather: *giving good advice.*
Bees, gather on a tree: *strengthening love and fidelity.*
Beehive, seeing: *delight and benefits.*
Beef, cut up, seeing: *receiving an inheritance.*
Beef, raw: (see under Meat)
Beer (cloudy), drinking or seeing: *illness and annoyance.*
Beer (clear), drinking or seeing: *steady health, cheerfulness and friendly meetings.*
Beer, spilled over: *indicates declining wealth.*
Beer barrel: *business is going well.*
Beer-house, pub: *beware of carelessness.*
Beer mug (tankard), seeing: *drinking is harmful.*
Beet, turnip, seeing: *happy family, prosperity, luck in love.*
Beet field, seeing: *coming into a huge fortune.*
Beetroot, seeing lots of: *getting into bigger ventures.*
Beetroot, nice, seeing on a field: *positive development of your plans.*
Beheaded, seeing yourself: *fear, affliction, loss of an influential sponsor.*
Beheaded, seeing someone: *overcoming enemies; return of a long missing friend.*
Bell, seeing: *ventures with risks.*
Bell-tower, seeing: *happiness, power, honor.*
Bells, hearing them ring: *a good omen for business contracts;* **for married couples:** *arguments, disagreements.*
Belly, having a big one: *being well off, comfort.*
Belly, a small one: *a long-lasting lawsuit.*
Belly, swollen: *misfortune, hidden secrets.*
Bellows: *squabble, discord.*
Belt, finding: *gaining trust.*
Belt, in silver: *confined wealth.*
Belt, losing: *neglected plans.*
Belt, or leash, in gold, seeing: *great riches and health.*
Belt, tearing apart: *disaster ahead.*
Belt, new, wearing: *forthcoming honor, soon to be engaged.*
Bench, seeing: *leading a peaceful life.*

Bending down: *degradation, harm.*
Berries, eating or searching: *hardship and grief.*
Bet, propose or agreeing to one: *uncertainty in business; losses ahead.*
Betting: *beware of risky speculation.*
Bigger, becoming; seeing yourself growing huge: *a rich marriage.*
Bile, vomiting: *anger, annoyance.*
Bill, seeing: *safe keeping of your documents.*
Billiard, playing or seeing: *doubtful venture, unstableness.*
Binding, something: *lawsuit matters*
Birds, singing: *joy with your children; your loved ones seem to be happy.*
Birds, flying: *continuation in business, prosperous success.*
Bird, in a cage: *secure assets.*
Birds, colorful or strange, seeing: *vulnerability in relations, regarding your friends.*
Bird's nest, finding: *experiencing plenty of joy.*
Bird's nest, empty: *annoyance, or tricks.*
Bird's nest, taking eggs from: *grief and trouble in your daily life.*
Birth, giving, seen: *coming into trouble.*
Birth, being born: *for poor people—good; for business people—a bad omen.*
Birth, with complications, attending: *losses, painful disgrace.*
Birth, giving to a boy: *prosperity in all undertakings.*
Birth, giving to a girl: *painful experiences being in a cheerful, joyful situation.*
Bishop, seeing: *favored by a dignitary.*
Bite, fear, from animals or to escape from: *jealousy.*
Bleaching something: *you will get justification.*
Bleeding: *falling into sadness.*
Blessings, receiving: *joy and happiness.*
Blind, becoming: *danger ahead.*
Blind, being yourself: *deceived by false friends.*
Blind people, guiding: *taking opportunities to help the needy.*
Blind people, seeing: *a hindrance, obstacles in undertakings.*
Blinking-eye, seeing: *huge gains.*
Blisters, removing a band-aid : *good health.*
Block (log), hitting: *someone insults you.*

Blood, dripping from you to the ground: *a good omen.*
Blood, collecting, picking up: *also a good sign.*
Blood, drinking: *is "good."*
Blood, rotten, foul, seeing: *severe illness.*
Blood, being carried: *is malicious and of evil.*
Blood, collecting from an animal: *big business ambition.*
Blood, seeing curdled: *suffer from illness.*
Blood, of a nice color: *cheerfulness in the days ahead.*
Blood, vomiting: *"wealth" for those who are poor.*
Blueberries, eating: *a struggling future ahead.*
Boar, seeing: *being frightened; being followed by rivals.*
Boar, seeing destroying crops: *disputes with friends.*
Boar, to kill—shoot: *victory over a rival, overcoming danger.*
Boar-wild, being attacked: *being held up by evil people.*
Board-game, playing or seeing: *uncertainty and doubtful success in business deals.*
Border, establishing: *money situation is improving.*
Boards, seeing: *flourishing business.*
Boat, a small one: *a forthcoming trip.*
Boat, a ferry, riding in, on sea or river, in clear water: *joy and success in all undertakings.*
Boat, sinking: *breakup of a love relationship.*
Body, deformation: *you will be shamed.*
Body, injuries: *being in trouble.*
Body, your own, exposing: *experiencing shame.*
Bolt (or lock), seeing: *annoyance kept secret.*
Bone marrow, finding in legs: *great wealth and happiness.*
Bone marrow in dumplings, preparing: *making a good living.*
Bones, seeing: *lots of work ahead.*
Bones, nibbling on: *worries about food shortage.*
Bonnet, putting on: *soon to be married.*
Bonnet and hats, seeing: *lingering disease.*
Boot, nice, in good quality: *coming to honor, and loyal servants.*
Books, buying: *usefulness to yourself and others.*
Books, learning from: *earning respect.*
Books, seeing: *experiencing the unexpected.*

Books, seeing burned: *hoped for joy ---loosing.*
Books, useful ones, reading: *privately speculating.*
Borrowing something: *free yourself of worrisome matters.*
Born, being: *for a needy person,* **good;** *for a well-off person,* **bad.**
Bottles, seeing broken: *means sadness.*
Bottles, cleaning: *coming into bad company.*
Bottle, seeing or having: *joy and fun.*
Bottom (buttocks), your own: *confusion in business.*
Bottom, seeing of a woman: *succumb to trivial matters, or a silly fuss.*
Bow, ribbon: *sliding into difficult situations.*
Bowl, dish, seeing: a *dinner invitation.*
Box, seeing: *discovering a secret.*
Box, losing one: *in a disagreement with yourself.*
Box, in silver, seeing: *good omen.*
Box, beautiful painted: *lots of fun.*
Box, with a portrait: *a soon pleasant acquaintance.*
Box-tree, shrub, seeing green: *affirmation of your hopes.*
Boys, seeing: *a family addition.*
Bracelets putting on: *a secret love.*
Bracelets, receiving as a gift: *a returning love.*
Braided hair: *soon to be united in love.*
Branches green, seeing: *your hopes are coming true.*
Brandy, spirits, drinking or seeing: *evil lust.*
Brass merchandise, seeing: *being cheated by someone.*
Bread, baking: *your undertakings are ending well.*
Bread, burned, seeing: *means irresponsibility.*
Bread, eating: *having loyal friends and getting more.*
Bread, eating while still warm: *becoming sick.*
Bread, turning bad: *inconsistent luck.*
Bread, being prepared: *for diligent people,* **good;** *lazy ones,* **bad.**
Bread, a nice loaf seeing: *receiving honor and wealth.*
Breast, exposing: *bashfulness, modesty.*
Breast, big and healthy: *enjoying a steady health.*
Breast, nursing a baby: *joy in your marriage.*
Breast, seeing from a woman: *continuation of being in love.*
Breast, hairy, seeing: *lots of happiness in love.*

Bricklayer, seeing: *laziness brings harm.*
Bride, seeing running: *means "death."*
Bride or groom, hugging: *being faithful, even from afar.*
Bride or groom, escorting to the altar: *peace of mind.*
Bridge, walking or driving over: *happiness in love and all undertakings.*
Bridge, walking under: *lots of obstacles but still reaching the goal.*
Bridge, seeing: *security in undertakings.*
Bridge, being built of stone: *durability in your undertakings.*
Bridge, being built of wood: *insupportable, in situations*
Bridge, seeing, collapse: *big interruptions in business.*
Bristles, seeing: *there are obstacles in your ventures.*
Broom: *unpleasantness and difficulties among friends.*
Brother or sister, talking or seeing: *annoyance, disagreements.*
Brother, walking away (death image): *disappearance of a powerful enemy.*
Brother, saying farewell to him: *sadness, depression.*
Broth, drinking: *business proceedings go well;* ***for an ill person****—a slow recovery; lovers will soon tie the knot.*
Broken pieces seeing: *all earthly things are transient.*
Brushing: *lots of fun is coming your way.*
Buck, stag killing: *a defeat of your enemies.*
Buckle: *continuation in business ventures.*
Building, seeing being demolished: *brushing obstacles aside.*
Building, nice and large: *new ventures, undertakings.*
Building, small, living in: *peace of mind about your destiny.*
Buffalo, seeing: *many casualties, and losses.*
Bull, seeing or being pursued: *risks, loosing a dear friend, unpleasantnesss from family members.*
Bullet, being hit by: *you will need doctor's care.*
Bullets, rolling in front of you: *ill-fated success.*
Bullets, flying into your house: *danger lies ahead.*
Bumps, swollen on your body: *getting a real estate.*
Burden, a heavy one: *depressions.*
Burdock, sticking on you: *a warning of obtrusive people.*
Buried being alive: *coming into great danger.*
Buried, seeing yourself: *health and long life.*

Burial, watching: *sorrow, discord, illness or disease.*
Burning, seeing: *forthcoming disaster.*
Burning glass, looking through: *errors, mistakes.*
Bushes, cutting up: *removing all obstacles out of love.*
Bushes (underbrush), seeing: *expect obstacles.*
Bushes, hiding behind: *danger at present.*
Businessman, seeing: *good progress in ventures.*
Butcher, seeing or talking to him: *being offended, loosing your lover.*
Butter, eating: *discord, conflict, annoyance with relatives.*
Butter, making: *inner calmness.*
Butterfly, seeing or catching: *unsteadiness, unfaithful.*
Buying, something: *extravagance brings disadvantage.*

C

Cabbage, seeing or eating: *unexpected grief, sorrow.*
Cabbage (Savoy), seeing or eating: *pretending to be happy; a show off.*
Cabinet-maker, visiting his shop: *discord in your matters, but sorting things out.*
Cage, cleaning out: *imprisonment, or other danger.*
Cage, emptying of birds: *release of affliction.*
Cake (torte), fancy: *revelry is harming your health.*
Cake, baking: *happiness, and prosperity.*
Calculate, without reading a result: *annoyance, cheating.*
Calendar, seeing: *achieving a better living standard.*
Calves, seeing: *unwise tricks.*
Calves, being killed: *recovery from an illness.*
Camel, seeing: *experiencing something out of the ordinary; becoming rich.*
Can (jug): *receiving good news.*
Can (jug), drinking from: *means great joy.*
Canary, seeing or hearing: *phony, empty compliments.*
Candlelight: *being protected from trouble.*
Candles, blowing out: *a breakup with an acquaintance.*
Candles, burning, carrying: *means death.*

Candles, seeing: *invitation to a happy occasion.*
Cannonball, seeing: *experiencing <u>sorrow.</u>*
Cannon discharge: *withstanding something repulsive.*
Canopy, seeing: *getting a position of dignity, joy.*
<u>**Canteen (kitchen),**</u> **woman working, talking or seeing:** *late —but not too late, coming out of a misery.*
Car: *(see under Vehicle).*
Cardinal of a church: *happiness and welfare.*
Card player, seeing: *escaping from danger.*
Card playing: *arguments, unhappy in love, late marriage.*
Card playing, showing lots of pictures: *favorable prospects, and a rich bride.*
Card playing, showing lots of hearts: *a happy, satisfying marriage and many children.*
Card tricks, magic: *seeking popularity.*
Cargo-wagon: *busy activity in your business.*
Carnations: *your descendants give you lots of joy.*
Carp, eating or seeing: *health improvement.*
Carpets: *fondness of luxury — waste brings decline in prosperity.*
Carriage (coach), riding in: *tendency being arrogant, that will lead to misery.*
Carriage (coach), stepping out: *loosing your dignitary position.*
Carrier, seeing: *anger, discord.*
Carrion animal, seeing: *good times, — long life.*
Case (box), yours, seeing: *stolen goods are being returned.*
Cash box, yours, seeing: *disadvantage in business.*
Castle, seeing: *a very good, joyful omen.*
Castle on fire: *disaster, illness.*
Cattle herd, seeing: *prosperity.*
Cattle, guiding: *immediate prosperity turning into bad luck.*
Cats seeing or having: *annoyance, persecution, cheated by lovers, or servants, in contact with false people, unaware of.*
Cats, being scratched or bitten by: <u>*coming in contact with evil people*</u>
Catching: *insidiousness; tricks.*
Caterpillar: *damage to your belongings.*
Cauliflower: *honor, and profit.*

Cave, dying in it: *low in your spirit, depressions.*
Caves, seeing or living in: *big changes in your luck and happiness.*
Celery: *beware of flattery.*
Cellar, seeing or being in: *sickness lies ahead.*
Cellar, sweeping: *bad business.*
Cellar steps, falling down: *a <u>prolonged; persistent, lingering disease.</u>*
Chain, seeing: *imprisonment; pursuit, outwitted by enemies; soon taking your bride to the altar.*
Chain, wearing: *bad, disastrous times ahead.*
Chain, being chained: *a position is being offered.*
Chair, beautiful, seeing: *promotion, a high position, wealth.*
Chair, dirty and worn out: *interruption or destroying family harmony.*
Chair of many colors, seeing: *happy times ahead.*
Chair in black, seeing: *indicating "death."*
Chair, sitting in: *unstable health.*
Chalk: *you will lose a lot of money.*
Chamomile, seeing: *you will live a very long life.*
Chandelier: *festivities lie ahead.*
Chapel, seeing: *joy; and loyal friends.*
Chaplain, becoming: *great honor.*
Charity, handing out: *deep gratitude, calmness, satisfaction.*
Charity, receiving: *changing luck.*
Charm, being charmed: *losing business deals.*
Charming someone: *becoming imprudent.*
Chasm, falling into, being swallowed up: *quick rescue from a danger.*
Cheek: *take better care about cleanliness.*
Cheeks, scratched and bony: *sadness and sorrow.*
Cheeks, big and red: *good prospect into the future.*
Cherry tree : *being in a good atmosphere.*
Cherries, eating or seeing: *pleasantness coming your way in different varieties.*
Cherries, sour, eating: *depression, or sorrow.*
Cheese, eating or seeing: *happiness and health.*
Chess game: *overall knowledge is the best investment.*
Chest (box), empty: *annoyance, misfortune.*
Chest (box), a full one: *plenty, abundance.*

Chest (furniture), buying or seeing: *enduring small losses.*
Chest, body, wounded: *for seniors--a bad omen; for youth –a good omen.*
Child, baby, wrapping nicely up: *happiness.*
Children falling down: *disruptions, often decline in business.*
Children, seeing: *joy; health; happiness; inner peace; happy marriage; success in all undertakings.*
Children at play: *joyfulness; cheerfulness; peace of mind.*
Childbirth seeing: *addition to the family, increasing prosperity.*
Chimney: *a good family life.*
Chimney sweep: *rescue from danger.*
China (dishes): *thirst for pleasure is wasting your life away,*
Chives: *trouble, damage in your undertakings.*
Choking: *you will be well soon.*
Christ, worshipping: *brings joy.*
Christ, seeing on the cross: *perish; ruin.*
Christ, hearing him speak: *cheerfulness.*
Church, seeing: *protection from evil and bad things to come.*
Church, praying in: *happiness; joy; progress in all good things.*
Church destroyed, or seen in ruins: *forthcoming disaster.*
Churchyard, seeing: *lingering illness; invalidism.*
Cigars, making: *good health.*
Cigar, smoking: *enjoyment and wealth.*
Circle seeing: *punctuality brings profit in business.*
City hall: *involvement in lawsuits.*
City, large, walking through: *vexation of all kinds, restlessness.*
City, small, friendly, seeing: *frugal; making a good living.*
City, with many high towers: *starting a grand operation, an enterprise.*
City, seeing destroyed: *misfortune, loss of honor and wealth.*
Clergyman, seeing or talking: *is comforting;* **but for the sick, or lovers** *—of bad consequences.*
Cliff, seeing: *your calculation is wrong.*
Climbing up a hill: *repulsiveness.*
Climbing a tree: *coming into dignity and honor; long courtship.*
Climbing a mast: *poverty and affliction.*
Clock, seeing: *be more aware of the <u>present.</u>*

Clothing, shabby, wearing: *poverty*
Closet, seeing: *sincerity pleases more than being reserved.*
Clouds, condensed, seeing on a mountain: *oppressive burdens.*
Clouds, black and heavy: *discord; arguments; misery.*
Clouds, falling down from: *huge embarrassments.*
Clover, seeing being planted: *happy family life.*
Clover, four-leafed, finding: *extraordinary luck.*
Clover field, lush and green: *a hopeful future.*
Clysters, seeing: *your business is proceeding well.*
Clysters (enema), getting: *riches; wealth.*
Clysters (applicator), seeing: *impenetrable business.*
Clucking (hen), seeing: *luck and blessings.*
Coach (carriage), riding in: *tendency to haughtiness; sure downfall; misery.*
Coach (carriage), stepping out: *losing trust and respectful position.*
Coal, seeing: *great wealth; and luck.*
Coal, seeing burning: *carefulness in choosing friends; all in all, be careful.*
Coal, wanted to eat: *misfortune, bad luck.*
Coal mine seeing: *marrying a widow.*
Coat of Arms seeing: *haughtiness.*
Coat, new, putting on: *terminating previous worries.*
Coat, too big, putting on: *sadness.*
Coat, wearing or seeing one: *reaching dignity.*
Coat, tearing: *separation.*
Coat, losing: *forthcoming misery.*
Coat, animal skin, tanner : *everybody is angry.*
Cock (chafer): *causing suspicion; distrust.*
Cockade, seeing or wearing: *courage, dignified behavior.*
Cockade, not yours, wearing: *treason and ingratitude.*
Coffee, seen or roasting: *misfortune, bad luck, persecution.*
Coffee grinding: *annoyance, trouble.*
Coffee house, visiting: *accident of a friend or relative.*
Coffin, seeing: *a long and happy life.*
Coins, precious metal: *considerable riches, lucky business deals.*
Colic, having: *sickness in the family.*

Colonnade, seeing, touring, walking: *riches, happiness.*
Color-paints in a box: *full cash register.*
Column (pillar) seeing: *coming to honor.*
Column (pillar), collapsing: *becoming an invalid; illness.*
Comb, seeing: *illness and worries.*
Comedy (play), seeing: *contempt, blasphemy.*
Comet, seeing: *price hike; war time; dying and torment; bad harvest; unexpected news.*
Comfort, receiving and not needing it: *a good omen.*
Communion (holy), receiving: *steady happiness; finding friends in troublesome times.*
Company, with them on horseback, or driven by: *tendency for waste and extravagance.*
Concert, attending: *grief, loss of relatives and friends.*
Confectionery (sweets), eating: *advantage, benefit.*
Conference or courtroom, attending a public meeting: *being in pursuit of political activities.*
Confessional: *disagreeableness, unpleasantness.*
Confessional (priest), or confessing: *regulating confused business.*
Conquest in war: *authority, prestige and honor.*
Contrabass, seeing: *dispute, arguments.*
Contrabass, being played: *unity, harmony.*
Convertible (car), driving: *joy and happiness.*
Cook, seeing: *unnecessary expenses*
Cookies, eating: *means, good times ahead.*
Cooking: *a fun and cheerful festivity lies ahead.*
Copper (money): *effortless work.*
Cord (chain), of gold, seeing: *profit; remarkable improvement of your assets.*
Coronation of a King or Queen, attending: *prosperous success at present; favorable situations.*
Corpse being buried: *lovers soon to be separated.*
Corpse, seeing: *indicates a wedding.*
Corpulence: *increasing your wealth.*
Corset (undergarment): *vanity, bringing deep sorrow.*
Cotton, waving: *gain, profit.*

Cotton shrub: *riches, wealth.*
Coughing: *your secrets are being revealed.*
Counterfeit: *shame, disgrace, misery.*
Court, being prosecuted: *confusion, perplexity.*
Courthouse, standing in front of one: *seeking your rights.*
Courtroom: *bad luck, repulsiveness.*
Cover, seeking from enemies: *indicates fraud.*
Cows, seeing: *success in ventures.*
Cow milk, drinking: *unstable health.*
Cow stable, being in one: *rescued from an illness.*
Cowl, a monks hood, seeing: *peace of mind, state of bliss.*
Crab, eating or seeing: *declining business, pain, disagreement.*
Cradle, seeing: *a bright future.*
Crane (bird), seeing: *bad omen; disaster; disloyal friends or servants.*
Cranes (birds), flying: *good news.*
Cranes (birds), crying: *means joy.*
Creditor, seeing or being visited by: *secure, but effortless business.*
Creek, with many fish: *a good inheritance.*
Creek, with blood flowing: *illness caused by blood vomiting.*
Creek, dried out: *poverty, lingering prolonging illness.*
Creek, clear water, running into your house: *increase of fortune and wealth.*
Creek, muddy, running into your house: *illness, grief, sadness.*
Creek, swelling water level: *growing assets; but also fast declining.*
Crescent, seeing: *secure food supply.*
Crib, (feed), seeing empty: *a badly paid work.*
Crib, (feed), a full one, seeing: *huge profit.*
Criminal (person), seeing: *disagreeable people.*
Crippled person seeing: *getting unexpected help.*
Crocodile, seeing: *a warning about false people around you.*
Crop (harvest), yellow without spikes: *your plans will succeed.*
Crop (harvest), beautifully green: *big hopes for an upcoming acquisition.*
Cross (holy), decorated with flowers: *happy family life.*
Cross (holy), seeing: *sorrow.*
Cross (holy), on your head: *defamation.*

Crossbow, stretching: *fear and trouble.*
Crossbow, breaking: *a good future.*
Crow (bird), crying: *receiving bad news.*
Crow (birds), many on a tree: *a get-together of relatives.*
Crow (bird), seeing: *indicates death.*
Crown, seeing or wearing: *wealth and honor.*
Crown of myrtle, seeing or wearing: *invitation to a wedding; or your own wedding.*
Crowned, being: *sadness.*
Cruelty, being abused: *you will be insulted.*
Crust (scab), on the head: *acquisition of a great wealth.*
Crutches, using: *losing your lover, clumsiness in undertakings.*
Crutches, used by others: *getting help, support from unknown friends.*
Crying: *(see under weeping).*
Cuckoo, seeing or crying: *joy and good health.*
Cucumber, eating, or seeing: *sickness ahead.*
Cuffs, on sleeves, wearing: *coming to honor.*
Cuffs, on sleeves, of lace: *privilege.*
Cuffs, on sleeves, dirty or with holes: *losing your job.*
Cup (mug), breaking: *death of an enemy.*
Cup, made of silver: *profit, gain.*
Cup, dropping: *nervousness, anxiety.*
Cup, nice painted one, breaking: *imminent misfortune.*
Cup (goblet), drinking from: *good times ahead, lots of fun at dinner parties.*
Cups (mugs), seeing: *surprised by an unexpected visitor.*
Currant (red berry), eating or seeing: *steadfast, perseverance.*
Currant (white berry): *satisfaction.*
Currant (blackberry): *unfaithfulness.*
Curl, ringlets, seeing: *true love.*
Curtain, seeing: *discovering a secret.*
Customs building seeing: *beware of cheaters.*
Cypress tree seeing: *sadness, declining business.*

D

Dagger, losing: *poverty.*
Dagger, holding in your hands: *joy and honor.*
Dagger, hitting a stranger: *luck in business.*
Dagger, bloodshed, seeing: *having secret sponsors.*
Dagger, feeling danger of life: *swamped with charities.*
Dagger, receiving from a dignitary: *great honor.*
Dagger, seen broken: *death, or disease.*
Dagger, seeing: *news receiving from friends.*
Dagger, pursuing a person: *victory over your enemies.*
Dagger, being hurt by: *getting favors from friends.*
Dairy production, visiting: *being happy in your occupation; getting rich; receiving honor; happy times on trips.*
Dam, working on it: *good progress in your project.*
Dancing: *unexpected good news from a distant friend.*
Dancing and falling: *humiliation, arrogance.*
Darkness, finding a way to the light: *rescue from great danger.*
Darkness, being in it: *misery, difficulty.*
Dates, (fruit), handing out: *you will be kissed.*
Dates, eating: *being favored by a woman.*
Dawn—rosy, seeing: *stormy days ahead.*
Dead, seeing yourself: *lots of joy.*
Dead, being, and coming back to life: *honor and happiness.*
Dead, seeing a friend: *receiving news from an estranged friend.*
Dead people, seeing: *abused by friends; losing your lover; losing out on a "horse deal."*
Dead bodies, digging up: *experiencing cruelty.*
Dead bodies, on a battlefield: *sorrow lies ahead.*
Dead body with a wreath, seeing: *lingering illness.*
Dead person, seeing, dining with him or her: *great honor.*
Dead people, seeing awaken: *a dispute about inheritance.*
Dead, being dead yourself: *late marriage, luck in ventures.*
Death-bed, open casket: *unexpected inheritance.*
Debt, paying off: *grief, worries.*
Deer, seeing: *in pursuit of an innocent person.*

Deer, seeing running: *means a quick start in your trade.*
Deer, shooting: *inheritance; honor; humiliating weak, fearful enemies.*
Deer herd, seeing: *many friendships.*
Deer hind, seeing: *wealth, prosperity and happiness.*
Dentist, seeing or talking to: *fraud and misfortune.*
Denuding yourself, exposing: *experiencing shame.*
Deprived, being: *losing a relative.*
Deserting your faith: *bad business deals; ruin.*
Despair: *hardship, repulsiveness.*
Devil, seeing: *bad luck; interruption in plans; being tricked by false people.*
Diadem, putting on: *losses, insults, offence.*
Diamonds, seeing: *false, phony luck.*
Diamonds, receiving: *annoyance, bad luck.*
Diamonds, eating: *happiness, reward, advantage.*
Diarrhea, having: *indicates health.*
Dice, seeing: *hostility, disagreeableness.*
Dice, playing: *happy event, marrying your chosen partner, wealth and honor.*
Dinner, being invited: *you are well respected.*
Dinner (food), smelling burnt: *unpleasant news.*
Dirt, seeing: *damage through slander.*
Dirty, seeing yourself: *illness.*
Dirty, making yourself: *happiness.*
Dishes, out of metal: *good marriage, or satisfaction.*
Dishes, breaking: *a brawl; dispute; feud.*
Dishes, seeing: *domestic twist, disagreement.*
Dispute, getting involved: *anxiety; fear.*
Distill—cork, seeing: *annoyance, trouble.*
Ditch, falling into: *caution about traps, falseness.*
Ditch, jumping over: *treason, unfaithfulness.*
Ditch, standing before a deep one: *great danger.*
Doctor, who bandaged up a relative: *impending marriage in the family.*
Doctor with a patient, having a friendly talk: *impending indisposition.*
Doctor, visits you: *privilege and happiness.*

Doctor, seeing: *for a sick person -* **health***; for a healthy person -* **death***.*
Documents, receiving: *promotion ahead.*
Dog, seeing a white one: *a pleasant acquaintance.*
Dogs seeing and playing with: *luck in business; reconciliation with those on bad terms, winning back estranged friends, truly being loved again.*
Dogs, your own, seeing: *great wealth.*
Dog, being attacked by: *approaching danger.*
Dogs seen, hunt, chase: *unsteadiness, excess.*
Dogs, fighting: *family discord about inheritance.*
Dogs, attacking you: *coming into danger.*
Doghouse: *decline in your social status.*
Dolphin, playing: *misfortune or even death.*
Domestic (servants): *lots of effort and work.*
Donation, handing out: *piece of mind, satisfaction.*
Donations, receiving: *change of luck.*
Donkey, buying: *austerity; profit.*
Donkey, hear the crying: *losses, damage and struggle.*
Donkey, hitting one: *being too hard-hearted towards your loved ones.*
Donkey, loaded with baggage: *increase of your wealth, prosperous ventures; all-round respect.*
Donkey, riding on: *slowly but surely reaching your goal.*
Donkey, seeing: *loyalty and obliging in your love; prosperous business.*
Door, burning or been destroyed: *dying friends or relatives.*
Dove, seeing: *pleasant news.*
Dove, catching: *annoyance.*
Doves flying: *good news, much luck in business.*
Dovecot: *peace and harmony.*
Drag, seeing: *many obstacles in your ventures.*
Dragon, flying: *pretended, untrue happiness.*
Drawbridge: *unexpected trip.*
Drawing (a sketch): *truthful friends.*
Dress closet: *luck and profit.*
Dress, fabric, seeing: *vanity causes heartbreak.*
Dress, having a nice one: *coming into good circumstances.*
Dress, stained: *sadness.*

Dresses, putting them on: *luck; good circumstances.*
Dresses, in white: *luck in love and all ventures.*
Dresses, in black: *sorrow; losing your lover; painful experiences.*
Dresses, blue or purple: *happiness; joy; prosperity; loyal friends.*
Dresses, in many colors: *inconsistency in happiness; annoyance by your lover; danger of loosing the friend or lover*
Dresses, in crimson color: *old age; honor; your love was a happy choice.*
Dresses, dark red: *losing suspicious friend, quarrelling about pedantry; annoyance from your children.*
Dresses, dirty, and torn: *difficulties in marrying the person you have chosen; losing friends.*
Dresses, from other nations: *a far trip ahead*
Dresses, in green: *preferred by your lover or suitors; advantageous offers.*
Dresses, in yellow: *falseness; jealousy; losing people who meant well.*
Dresses, tearing apart: *annoyance ahead; anger.*
Dresses, washing: *becoming economical, saving is recommended.*
Dressing gown, wearing: *indisposition experiencing.*
Drink, given to you: *an invitation will be received.*
Drink, mixing: *imminent sickness in the family.*
Drinking glasses, decorative: *getting out of a bad situation.*
Drinking fresh water: *a good omen.*
Drinking from a glass: *risk; revealing secrets.*
Drinking vinegar: *discord, dissension of family members.*
Drinks: *beware of your enemies.*
Driving and turning over: *forthcoming accident.*
Driving, seen: *envy, jealousy.*
Driving, in a car or carriage to a wedding or baby christening: *having honor and power, especially when a carriage is pulled by people, without getting hurt.*
Drowning: *prosperity and happiness.*
Drowning, watching: *triumph, victory over your enemies.*
Drowned, being by someone else: *losses of all kinds.*
Drum (drummer): *enduring small losses.*
Drunk, being: *finding unexpected, unknown friends.*
Drunk people, seeing: *repulsiveness, abhorrence.*

Drunkenness, being addicted: *happiness and health.*
Duck, nice one: *great honor;* ***for slanderous people -*** *losses and sorrow.*
Ducks, catching: *success in receiving approval or acceptance.*
Ducks, trying to catch: *casualties.*
Ducks, swimming: *overcoming bad gossips.*
Ducks, wild geese, flying: *a joy-bringing message.*
Duel, participating in: *impending danger of death.*
Dumb person, seeing: *charity brings blessings.*
Dumplings, eating or making: *gossip will bring harm.*
Dwarf (gnome): *being persuaded by weak enemies.*
Dying: *receiving many empty promises.*

E

Eagle, your own: *strength in your intentions.*
Eagle, flying high in circles: *prosperity; wealth; honor; happiness in love.*
Eagle, sitting on your head: *means a death case.*
Eagle, standing or sitting on you: *for rich people -* *death;* ***for the poor*** *- only good.*
Earth, talking to: *very good, huge wealth and prosperity.*
Earth, seeing split apart: *forthcoming danger.*
Earthquake, feeling: *changes; uncertainty; unstable future.*
Earth - soil, black: *annoyance; misfortune; affliction.*
Earth - ground, yellow, glowing: *happiness; success; loyal friendship.*
Earth - soil, being worked: *family addition.*
Earthworms, seeing: *influential; powerful enemies.*
Ears, beautiful or extremely large: *seeing a friend -- happy.*
Ears, pulling: *unfair treatment, suppressed hopes.*
Ears, like a donkey seeing: *being abused.*
Ears, cleaning: *loyal servants.*
Earrings, wearing or seeing: *treason, effortless work.*
Eating, seeing others: *an invitation.*
Eating, yourself: *difficulties with your loved ones; misfortune in business; annoyance in love; arguments and trouble.*

Eclipse seeing: *losing many friends through defamation; getting a bad reputation.*
Eel, removing from water: *for the sick - health; for the healthy - goodness.*
Eel, seeing stripped: *for prisoners – freedom, being free - help out of misery.*
Eel, seeing dead: *sorrow and annoyance.*
Eggs, belonging to you: *gain, harmony in the family.*
Eggs, seen broken: *losses; arguments; poverty; separation from friends or lovers.*
Eggs, eating: *becoming a father; happiness.*
Eggs, dropping: *disharmony.*
Eggs, finding: *becoming a bride or groom.*
Eggs, open and rotten: *bad reputation.*
Eggs, red, seeing: *anger; fire; death of a friend.*
Eggs, seeing or buying: *much success in business; promotion; improving prosperity; good children; old age.*
Eggs, seeing in yellow: *serious illness.*
Elder – shrub: *recovery from an old, lingering health problem.*
Elephant, seen, being killed: *your plans are being destroyed.*
Elephant, killed by you: *indicates your death.*
Elephant, seeing: *big plans; luck in business deals; late, but a good marriage.*
Embroider (embroidery): *reaching for the unthinkable; being a slave in awe.*
Emperor and kings, seeing: *lots of luck.*
Endive, or other greens, eating: *difficulties.*
Enemy, meeting: *overcoming unpleasantness; defeating rivals; strengthening your position; overcoming all troubles.*
Engagement: *growing family.*
Engagement time: *reverence; veneration; worship.*
Englishman, seeing or talking to: *false friends, bad creditors.*
Entertainment - amusement: *losses of all kinds.*
Ermine, putting on, wearing: *happiness and great wealth.*
Escape, being of help: *because of your goodness; you earn inconvenience, trouble and difficulties.*

Escaping: *avoiding danger.*
Essences (perfume), using: *unfaithfulness, being cheated in general.*
Estate, inheriting: *becoming a bride or groom.*
Estate, buying: *return to being well-off again.*
Estate, selling: *decline in economic activity.*
Estate your own and beautiful: *ability to have peace.*
Estate, countryside, getting: *unexpected inheritance.*
Estate, country, cultivating: *lots of activities.*
Evergreen, seeing or picking: *loyal friendship.*
Execution, attending: *dubious success in ventures.*
Execution-place, going to or seeing: *happiness and honor.*
Executioner, seeing: *forthcoming expulsion.*
Exile, being sent: *great love;* **for an ill person -** *health.*
Exile, received as a judgment: *changing views about business.*
Eyebrows, falling out: *imminent disaster.*
Eyebrows seeing in black: *health.*
Eyelids, big and beautiful: *honor and respect.*
Eyeglasses, sunglasses, wearing: *caution about friends.*
Eyes, bad, weak: *losses of all sorts, short on money.*
Eyes, being robbed of them: *shattered hopes, losing a good friend, unpleasantness in love.*
Eyes, beautiful, your own: *happiness and riches.*
Eyes, good vision: *you have good people around you.*
Eyes, squinting: *humiliating yourself.*
Eyes, dripping wet: bad future, losing your good reputation.

F

Fabric (garment), buying or seeing: *lucky projects.*
Face, covering: *bad, serious news.*
Face, seeing refined in a mirror: *your wishes being fulfilled.*
Face, your own, beautiful: *proceeding in projects and plans.*
Face, your own, ugly, seeing: *many worries, and sorrow.*
Face, ugly, reflect in water: *enmity, hostility.*
Face, beautiful, seeing in water: *long life.*

Face, meeting a beautiful one: *means much joy.*
Face, seeing pale: *sickness; or death.*
Face, putting on makeup: *woman who doesn't need it - good; for man - mockery; ridicule and despise.*
Face, without a nose: *means death.*
Face washing: *remorse, repentance.*
Factory (company), your own: *flourishing business.*
Fair, a market place: *communication with many people.*
Fainting: *unpleasant news.*
Fairy, seeing or talking to: *great luck in all matters of life.*
Falcon, golden: *great honor.*
Falcon, flying: *being cheated or deceived.*
Falling from a high place: *disaster; loss of honor; respect, and your fortune.*
Falling, but holding on: *be saved or protected from bad luck.*
Falling over an obstacle: *getting information.*
Falling and being hurt: *many conflicts.*
Fan, a hand-fan, held: *betrayal.*
Farewell: *loyalty; friendship.*
Farmer, seeing: *luck and happiness.*
Farmyard, seeing: *a rich inheritance.*
Fat, lard, eating: *means illness.*
Feet, seeing, not attached to a body: *imminent danger.*
Feet, sore: finding support for your business.
Feet, washing: *becoming excessive; getting sick; suffering.*
Fence, seeing: *others want to see you in chains, handcuffed.*
Festivities, attending: *painful news; sorrow.*
Fat, stout becoming: *means unexpected wealth.*
Fat, or oil, cooking: *indicates losses.*
Fat, plump children, your own: *good years are ahead.*
Father, becoming: *worrisome, but experiencing good times.*
Father, of many children: *increasing worries.*
Feast, attending: *unpleasantness; worries; discord in love, annoyance with children.*
Feathers, covered by: *interruptions in business undertakings.*
Feathers, black seeing: *recession in business, annoyance.*

Feathers, taking: *means honor.*
Feathers, white, own: *being cleared of false suspicions.*
Feather-quill, and writing: *soon receiving good news.*
Feathers, white: *welfare and amusement.*
Feathers, seeing many, flying: *hoped for luck, in vain.*
Feeding animals: *good progress in projects.*
Feet, broken: *receiving pity, because of an accident.*
Feet, which are deformed: *suffer from ignorance.*
Feet, having them dirty: *nasty sickness ahead.*
Fever having: *unsteady love and friendship.*
Fever, others been affected: *happiness in marriage; having peace of mind without wealth.*
Field, green and beautiful: *hope of good earnings; happy in love and marriage, wealth; honor; in prospect of a prosperous position.*
Field, seeing uncultivated: *stagnant plans.*
Field, working over: *being active; keeping yourself busy.*
Field, lay waste: *falling into sadness.*
Field, seeing destroyed by hail: *false speculation.*
Field, in beautiful bloom: *success of your hopes.*
Field, running through, or on horseback: *soon receiving a message from the person you await.*
Field, planting and sowing: *when courting a woman and want children* - *good; for others* **-** *means work, illness and displeasure.*
Fig, eating or seeing: *happiness in marriage and love.*
Figs, receiving as a gift: *friendly behavior.*
Fig tree, seeing: *being shielded, protected.*
Fight: *(see under Battle).*
Fighting: *having a dispute, arguments.*
Fighting on horseback: *getting a rich woman from a good family.*
Fighting wild animals and defeat: *being rescued from great danger.*
Fighting-fencer: *frustration about your hopes; separation or loss of a lover.*
Fighting, winning a prize: *happy ending in started ventures.*
File (office), receiving: *warning information about enemies.*
Finding money or other things: *your worries will soon be over.*
Fine, paying: *means advantage.*

Finger, burned: *falling into temptation.*
Finger, cut and bleeding: *luck in love.*
Finger, losing: *indicates harm or damage.*
Finger, very nice, seeing: *respect and honor.*
Fingernails, long and nice: *wealth, honor, a good wife, unexpected money.*
Finger ring, losing / giving away: *suffer, and lingering illness.*
Finger ring, receiving: *great honor.*
Fire (blaze), seeing: *unconditional love, wealth, your children are being blessed.*
Fork, seeing: *being deceived.*
Fortress, seeing: *unexpected opposition, hostility, also illness.*
Fortress, (ruins) seeing: *means sadness.*
Fortress (ruins), climbing up: *fearless in any danger.*
Fortress ruins, falling down from: *being harmed.*
Fire, blowing out: *abandon projects and plans.*
Fire engine: *danger lies ahead.*
Fire engines, driving fast: *imminent misfortune.*
Fire, falling from sky: *experiencing hardship.*
Fire, falling into: *great losses, ill humor.*
Fire, more buildings in flames: *forthcoming honor; much goodness.*
Fire, huge, houses burn, in smoke and ashes: *disaster of all kinds, first by family members.*
Fire, dropping: *bad omen.*
Fire, seeing it go out on a stove: *for the sick - means death.*
Fire, small, on your stove: *great riches, wealth.*
Fire, running over it: *annoyance.*
Fire, running away from it: *vexation ahead.*
Fire, pail to extinguish: *forthcoming danger.*
Fire, burning bright: *being loved and not knowing it.*
Fire, lighting, but not burning: *not being loved.*
Fire signs, in the sky: *rising cost of living; enemy invasion; a lot of misery.*
Fireworks, seeing: *happiness.*
Fish, catching: *negligence.*
Fish, big, buying or seeing: *luck and advantage.*

Fish, seeing: *bad profit; sadness; illness; annoyance.*
Fish, fried, eating: *forthcoming prosperity.*
Fish, seeing being sold: *unpleasant entertainment.*
Fish, small, buying or eating: *losses of all kinds.*
Fish, slippery, seeing: *a hope for profit diminishes; or unfaithfulness.*
Fish, receiving as a gift: *showered with fake honors.*
Fish pond: *avoid sloppiness and dirtiness.*
Fishing gear, tackle, seeing: *fraud, persecution.*
Flag, carrying: *you will be honored.*
Flag, flying in the wind: *danger, bad luck ahead.*
Flames, clear and bright: *receiving money; or jewelry as a gift.*
Flax, beautiful, seeing: *frugal in your household.*
Flax, spin to nice threats: *finding good accommodation.*
Flattering, caress: *mean; evil; nasty.*
Fleas, on you: *overcome your enemies.*
Fleas, many, bitten by: *misfortune; poverty; difficulties.*
Fleet, naval, full sails: *imminent changes.*
Flies (insects), many: *having enemies; being stalked; grief and insult.*
Flies, killing: *hostility; eliminating of unpleasant things.*
Flood, high tide: *disagreements with people around you, or family members.*
Flood, seeing: *losses of all kinds.*
Floor, in different patterns, seeing, or walking on: *great satisfaction through sorrow and joy.*
Flour, seeing: *a death case.*
Flour, roasting: *unexpected misfortune.*
Flower bucket: *joy, instantaneous satisfaction.*
Flowers, beautiful: *much joy.*
Flowers, receiving as a gift: *honorable days.*
Flowers, picking, binding together: *soon to be engaged.*
Flowers, planting: *performing an act of kindness.*
Flowers, scattered: *negligence, recklessness.*
Flowers, tearing up: *someone is spoiling your happiness.*
Flute, playing: *disagreements, losses.*
Flying and falling down: *inconvenience.*
Flying, long distance: *pleasant days ahead; luck in ventures, praise.*

Flying towards heaven: *for servants - good; for others - a trip; for the sick - death.*
Flying, from a high perch: *arrogance.*
Fog: *(see under Mist).*
Fools, seeing, or talking to: *being cheated.*
Foolish, being crazy: *remarkable business success.*
Foolishness, craziness by friends or loved ones: *reconciliation with enemy, attachment, great mentors.*
Footbridge, over water: *being frightened.*
Footpath, narrow, walking: *don't leave the path of virtues; it is the only way to happiness.*
Forehead, high and wide: *concern about decision-making in your business, use your head !!!*
Forehead, narrow and small: *you must show courage.*
Forehead, wounded: *treason, finding out about it.*
Forest, seeing: *a pleasant winter lies ahead.*
Forest, walking in, or logging: *happy marriage; peace of mind; receiving good fortune.*
Forest, on fire: *enduring great losses.*
Forest, endless walk, with great effort: *defamation, pursuit, deceived by friends.*
Forester's house: *being well accepted on a trip.*
Forest ranger, meeting: *imminent mischief.*
Forge (iron), seeing: *getting plenty of work.*
Forge, hammer, hearing: *you will hear something pleasant.*
Forget-me-not, flowers: *you will be well remembered.*
Fortress, under fire: *war times.*
Fountain, seeing: *a merry festivity ahead.*
Fox, chasing or killing: *getting to know false friends and their tricky intentions.*
Foxes, creeping, crawling: *secret enemies thinking of bringing you down.*
French horn, musical instruments, seeing: *pleasant news.*
Friend, seeing deceased: *unexpected novelty news; postponing marriage.*
Friend, seeing, welcoming: *to reach fame and honor.*

Friends, insulting: *disdain.*
Friends, joking around with: *separation.*
Frighten, terrified: *danger, bad luck.*
Frills, ruffles, seeing: *vanity gets you in deep affliction or sorrow.*
Frogs, seeing in a pond: *plenty of money; lucky business; loyal love; married couple blessed with children; pleasant company on trips.*
Frogs, catching or killing: *suicide, harming yourself.*
Frogs, hearing them croak: *praise and fame.*
Frostbite: *carefulness in all activities.*
Fruit, handing out: *finding mentors and friends.*
Fruit in baskets, seen in storage: *a good omen.*
Fruit tree: *good continuation in your new business.*
Fruits, seeing: *beware of opponents, forthcoming unpleasantness.*
Fruit, sour, eating: *misfortune and illness.*
Fruit, sweet, eating: *great fortune, happiness.*
Frying pan, seeing: *means harm, injury.*
Frying, and rotating: *bad luck and pursuit.*
Funeral, arranging: *for a married couple -* family addition; *for single persons -* impending marriage; *for servants -* promotion.
Funeral, attending: *late marriage, mishap or death of a friend or relative.*
Funeral - procession, seeing: *unexpected inheritance.*
Funnel: *don't reach for the unattainable.*
Fur, receiving as a gift: *getting to know many mentors.*
Fur, seeing, or wearing: *progress in your occupation, or trade, gaining respect.*
Fury, bewitched people: *anger, rage, hate, enmity.*

G

Gable, seeing collapse: *accident, death.*
Gallnut, oak apple, eating or finding: *culminate, slander.*
Galley (slave): *courage, boldness.*
Gallows, seeing: *false friends, misfortune, unrest.*
Gallows, going to be hanged: *coming to honor.*

Game of forfeits: *distraction, a disadvantage to your business.*
Game (venison): *war; starvation; discord by lovers; dishonest friends.*
Game (venison), meat, eating: *prosperity.*
Gamble, with money: *quarrel, dispute.*
Garden, neglected, disorganized: *being surrounded by false advisors.*
Garden, beautifully landscaped, walking through: *enjoying amusements; growth of investments; forthcoming honor; good projects.*
Garden, high-fenced, seeing: *denial of a request.*
Garlic smell: *repulsiveness, adversity.*
Garment, buying: *means happiness.*
Garter, wearing or seeing: *bad luck, annoyance.*
Gate, seeing open: *your visitors are welcome.*
Gauze, on hat or arm, wearing: *sad, mournful message.*
Gazebo with Jasmine flowers: *means an engagement.*
Geese, seeing fly: *losses enduring.*
Geese, seeing: happiness; *great wealth; absent friends seeing soon.*
Geese, killing: *little pity for the needy.*
Gem, jewel, seeing: *falling into temptation.*
Gem, your own: *attain great honor.*
Gem, jewel, receiving: *increasing your wealth.*
Gem, jewel, wearing: *arrogance.*
Ghost, seeing: *temptation to sin; danger; losing lover or friend; receiving news of a death.*
Giant, seeing: *good omen, success in business.*
Gift, giving: *forthcoming new and honest friends.*
Gift, receiving: *dealing with difficulties.*
Gingerbread, eating: *pure joy.*
Girl, seeing: *experiencing challenges.*
Glass, breaking: *disaster; fright; panic; death of loved relatives.*
Glass, bursting while holding it: *separation.*
Glass, cutting: *something to be investigated.*
Glass, giving as a gift: *being well and fondly remembered.*
Glass, seeing: *uncertainty in business, doubtful success.*
Glide: *beware of allurement.*
Globe, seeing or having: *going on a big trip; soon to be happily married.*
Glory, well deserved: *be careful about flatterers.*

Gloves, having: *diminishing suspicions.*
Gloves, seeing or putting on: *honor and happiness*
Glowing (fire), warming yourself: *quarrel with a friend.*
Goat, he-goat, seeing jumping: *manipulation; playing tricks.*
Goat, he-goat, being pushed by: *arguments ahead.*
Goats, seeing: *means comfort.*
Goblet (cup), drinking from: *lots of fun at dinner party; good times ahead.*
God, hearing him talk: *joyfulness.*
God, praying to him: *tremendous joy.*
God, praising: *means suffering.*
God, seeing or talking to him: *worries and grief.*
God, worshipping, attending mass: *peace of mind, calmness.*
God, worshipping, you celebrating mass: *hard and depressive work ahead.*
Going astray: *many difficulties.*
Goiter, seeing: *immoderateness makes you sick.*
Gold bars, receiving: *unpleasantness, annoyance.*
Gold (coins), seeing or getting: *being truly loved, soon to be married.*
Goldfinch - bird: *interesting acquaintance.*
Goldfish: *obstacles in business ventures.*
Gold, giving as a present: *attending a wedding.*
Gold, losing: *being robbed, or cheated in business.*
Gold - mine, discovering: *a sure gain, definite profit.*
Gold, using as currency: *separation of friends, misfortune in ventures.*
Gold, seeing or own: *means flourishing success in started business.*
Gold, stealing: *losing respect, or your lover.*
Gold and silver dishes, seeing: *a flatterer is near you.*
Gold, wearing: *fickleness, inconstancy.*
Gooseberry, eating or seeing: *getting a grouchy husband or nagging wife.*
Goose eggs: *you find your good food.*
Goose meat, eating: *lots of happiness.*
Gorge, ravine, falling into: *a bad omen.*
Gospel: *receiving good advice and sympathy.*
Gout pain: *forthcoming danger, experiencing unpleasantness.*

Grain, crop cutting: *indicates joy.*
Grain-crop field, harvesting: *huge earnings.*
Grain-crop field, seeing: *luck in love and ventures.*
Grain-crop, receiving: *joy, profit, gain.*
Grain, wheat-spikes, a wreath wearing: *great honor.*
Grain-spikes, picking: *flourishing business.*
Grandchildren, your own: *everlasting well-being.*
Grandparents, seeing or talking: *a good plan carrying out.*
Grapes, seeing in: blue - *bad luck;* **white -** *joy;* **red -** *affliction.*
Grapes, bunches cutting: *unexpected separation.*
Grapes, getting as a present: *acquaintance.*
Grape-harvest, celebration: *happiness; honor; riches.*
Grass, seeing: *be alert about profiteers.*
Grasshopper, seeing: *happiness is of a short duration.*
Grass cutting: *good times ahead, wealth.*
Grater: *being pursued by evil people.*
Grave, climbing in: *false friends; defame; pursuit.*
Grave, climbing out of it: *being lucky in ventures, receiving gifts, late marriage.*
Grave, closing up with soil: *regaining your health.*
Grave, preparing: *losing a friend.*
Grave, seeing being prepared: *death of a relative.*
Grave, someone is being carried out: *helping a friend; a friend becomes your beneficiary.*
Grave, seeing: *discord; grief; postponed marriage.*
Grave, with green grass: *hope and wishes coming true.*
Gravedigger, seeing: *becoming sick.*
Green peas, seeing or collecting: *prosperity; cheerfulness; increasing your fortune.*
Green-peas, eating: *luck in ventures.*
Green-peas, planting: *hope in succeeding of an undertaking.*
Green-peas, nice, clean, seeing bloom: *means good progress in your new start.*
Greeted, being: *is bad.*
Groom to be, or thinking to become: *disaster; loss of a friend or lover.*
Grove, seeing: *going astray.*

Grouse, white, seeing flying: *unexpected news.*
Guarantor, becoming: *for the ill -* *good;* **for the healthy -** *lots of expenses.*
Guarantor, acceptance: *big disadvantage.*
Guard, seeing: *be careful with whom you are acquainted.*
Guests, accommodate: *friendship being returned.*
Guests, bid farewell: *separation from a favored thing.*
Guests, welcoming: *soon to have visitors.*
Guests, foreigner, stranger, shelter: *unexpected happiness.*
Guilty, being: *for the ill -* *death;* **for the healthy -** *a bad omen.*
Guinea fowl: *saving; modesty; leads to a worry-free retirement.*
Guitar, playing or hearing: *a happy party is coming up.*
Guns, seeing: *repulsiveness.*
Gun powder: *being drawn to a dangerous gang. .*
Gypsy: *beware of foolish tricks.*

H

Hail, damage caused: *disaster and illness.*
Hailstorm, seeing: *unpleasantness; annoyance; treason; wishes and hopes seen diminish.*
Hair, being braided: *connections trying to make.*
Hair curls, seeing: *becoming arrogant.*
Hair combing: *luck in all business activities, dissolving disagreements.*
Hair, entangled: *family quarrels.*
Hair, in grey, having: *burdened with worries.*
Hair, having in red: *you have enemies.*
Hair, losing: *going through bad times.*
Hair, styled: *a jolly party lies ahead.*
Hair, nice in black, seeing: *means health.*
Hair, not wearing your own: *forthcoming sickness.*
Hair, to have or see a braid: *old things are not always the best things.*
Hair, long, seeing: *being loved and respected.*
Hair, cut off: *ease about your worries.*
Hair, having cut off: *getting out of adverse matters.*

Hairdresser, seeing or talking to: *jet (? yet) to come – "distress."*
Hall, bright, "grand" and dancing: *great joy about a reconciliation.*
Hall, beautifully furnished: *coming into your desired living standard.*
Halberd, seeing: bloody fight, bloodshed.
Ham, eating: *having many children; forthcoming wealth.*
Ham, seeing: *reward and bonuses.*
Hammer, seeing: *brutal treatment, hard labor.*
Hammer, using to work with: *good progress in your work.*
Hand, amputating: *disaster ahead.*
Hand-basket, holding: *worries about the future.*
Handcuffed, being: *indicates cheating.*
Handkerchief: *cleanliness is good for your health.*
Hands, being wounded or dirty: *disadvantage; despise.*
Hands, swollen: *being unsociable, quarrelsome.*
Hands, washing: *to be honored.*
Hang, seeing a person: *receiving an honor.*
Hanging, to witness one: *forthcoming illness.*
Hanging, seeing yourself: *misfortune is imminent.*
Hanging yourself, or being hanged: *fear and misery ahead.*
Harbor, seeing: *delightful news, happiness and honor.*
Harm, endure: *being honored.*
Harness, wearing: *rage leads to nastiness.*
Harrow: *losses and illness.*
Harp, seeing or playing: *disappointment.*
Harpist, a female: *beware of reckless company*
Harvest, good, being present: *your wishes soon to be come true.*
Harvest, bringing home: *inheritance awaits you.*
Harvesting in bad weather: *is a bad omen.*
Hat, wearing, nice looking: *advantage, luck and recognition.*
Hawk, seeing: *jealousy.*
Hay, bad smelling, rotten: *disruption in business.*
Hay wagon: *effort brings progress.*
Hazelnuts, cracking: *obtain a good profit.*
Head, another person's cut off: *good ventures ahead.*
Head, amputated: *falseness, fraud from people around you.*

Head-band: *occupying yourself with vanity; makeup and attire are defacing you.*

Head, bald, seeing: *experiencing slander.*

Head, extremely large, carrying: *triumph over your enemies, honor and dignity ahead.*

Head of a colored person, seeing: *good news from distant friends or relatives.*

Head, shaving: *dangerous, serious illness.*

Head, without body, seeing: *happiness and blessings.*

Head, washing: *avoiding a disaster.*

Head with tangled hair: *twists and quarrel ahead.*

Hearing loss: *means carelessness.*

Heart, bleeding: *offence, insult.*

Heart, cutting up: *separation of a loving couple.*

Heart, eating: *making sure your love is been returned.*

Heart, seeing: *tender loving.*

Hedgehog, seeing: *your goodness is being used negatively.*

Heel, injured: *bad luck of all kinds.*

Hell as described, seeing, being in it: *changes coming soon; suggested caution in all undertakings.*

Hell, being rescued from: *peace, courtesies, support.*

Hemp, tied together: *union is near.*

Hemp, spin: *activities in your household.*

Hen, big and nice, seeing: *happiness in loving.*

Hen, hearing one cluck: *a good and rich marriage.*

Hen ladder, seeing: *effort leads to prosperity.*

Hen, listen to squealing: *disaster, annoyance.*

Hen, seeing: *forthcoming insult, offence.*

Hen, with chicks, seeing: *lots of children, grandchildren, overall a large family.*

Herbs, eating: *long life.*

Herbs, searching for: *mischief, gain.*

Herd, seeing on prairie or meadows: *a happy future.*

Herring, eating: *avoid "drinking parties."*

Hermit, seeing: *grief and worries.*

Hip, having a big one: *being blessed with descendants.*

Hitting someone: *you have to defend yourself.*
Hole in your dress, seeing: *carelessness.*
Hole, crawling in: *coming into hostile company.*
Home, or apartment: *changes will come your way.*
Honey, eating: *discomfort, misery.*
Hood, seeing: *meeting a big fool.*
Hop-culture: *your ventures will prosper.*
Horn twisting: *getting out of a tricky situation.*
Hornet: *news is bringing a lot of unrest and confusion.*
Horns, having yourself: *to be fooled.*
Horns, from livestock, seeing: *is not good at all.*
Horseback rider, being thrown off: *experiencing humiliation in your pride.*
Horseback rider: *honor and dignity.*
Horseback rider, dismount: *losing a friend.*
Horseback rider, mount: *prosperity.*
Horse, seeing bolt: *coming into danger of death through carelessness.*
Horse, tumbling, or falling: *soon to encounter misfortune; bad luck.*
Horse harness: *pleasant, worry-free life.*
Horses, seeing or own: *happiness, lots of joy.*
Horses, seeing in front of a carriage: *soon to expect noble visitors.*
Horses, starved, seeing: *losing your good reputation.*
Horse stable: *effort and patience lead to your goals.*
Horse tail: *dignity, distinction.*
Horseshoe, seeing: *soon to go on a trip.*
Horseshoe, being present when put on: *efforts and hard work.*
Horse, being stubbed: *losing your lover.*
Hospital: *experiencing disgrace and shame.*
House, being built: *luck in business and love, good and loyal servants.*
House, being in it, and leaving: *gain, profit, advantage.*
House, being demolished: *getting rid of an obstacle.*
House, climbing up: *happiness; triumph; victory.*
House, falling from, deep down: *careful in all deeds.*
Household items, seeing a lot: *happiness in your marriage.*
House old burning, or collapsing: *disaster, unexpected case of death, losing your lover.*

House, old, seeing: *long time friends seeing again.*
Hound: *bad business deals.*
Hourglass, seeing: *a reminder, your lifespan on earth is limited.*
Howling, hearing: *experiencing slander.*
Human feces (stool), seeing: *means great wealth.*
Human feces, stepping into: *getting an unexpected large fortune.*
Hungry, being: *diligence and economy are the results of prosperity and honor.*
Hunt: *through perseverance a happy future lies ahead.*
Hunter: *a lot of effortless work.*
Hunting, deer: *plans and projects are ruined.*
Hunting, huge gems: *means great success in ventures.*
Hurricane, violent storm seeing: *losing your fortune.*
Hut, a cabin, seeing or being in it: *means hard work.*
Hyacinth: *receiving a gift.*
Hymn, singing or hearing: *a festivity will soon take place.*

I

Ice, seeing or gliding on: *accident is near; pursuit; cheated in love; scattered hopes.*
Ice, seeing in summer: *no use in starting anything.*
Icicles, hanging from your roof: *your love for each other grows deeper.*
Island, seeing or being there: *abandoned by friends.*
Illumination, seeing: *funny, joyful days ahead.*
Imperfection, experiencing: *effort and work in vain.*
Imprisonment: *comforting friends.*
Infantry, seeing: *price hikes, bad times.*
Infirmary, military hospital, being present: *long-lasting illness.*
Inheritance, receiving: *misery and grief.*
Ink, seeing: *reconciliation with your enemy.*
Ink, spilling over: *discord experiencing.*
Ink pot, overturning: *hostility and repulsiveness.*
Ink, writing with: *starting a new business.*
Insane people, seeing: *anger and revenge.*

Inscription on graves, reading: *loosing a family member.*
Insects, seeing: *gossip; illness; losses.*
Instruments, musical: *misadventure, death of a relative or acquaintance.*
Intestines, seeing: *means, joy and love.*
Insulted, being ill-treated: *annoyance and disagreement with household member.*
Intoxicated, being yourself: *avoiding excessiveness.*
Invalidity: *caution; illness.*
Itching, the skin: *you are about to make a mistake.*
Iron, seeing, or ironing: *a lot of troublesome work.*
Ivory, seeing: *indicates poverty.*

J

Jail, being in it: *exaltation.*
Jail, seeing one: *damaging to your health.*
Jaundice: *great wealth, unexpected good fortune.*
Jewish person, seeing or dealing with: *betrayal, deception.*
Jewish person, receiving service from: *unexpected luck; advantage in all matters.*
Jewelry, seeing or wearing: *a nice gift awaits you.*
Joy, experiencing: *beware of foolishness.*
Joyful, being in your sleep: *restlessness.*
Jubilate, a shout of joy: *disaster and sadness.*
Judge, seeing or talking to: *boring business.*
Judgment, being heard: *receiving unpleasant news.*
Judging, execution witnessing: *false love, unfaithfulness.*
Jug, a pitcher: *luck, joy; avoiding danger.*
Juggler, seeing: *beware of fraud.*
Juice, handing to a sick person: *privilege.*
Juice, squeezing: *worries about the future.*
Jumping into water: *danger, losing a friend or acquaintance.*
Jumping over a ditch, creek or fence: *overcoming imminent danger, avoiding a hostile plot.*
Juniper seeing: *evil gossip.*

K

Kettle, seeing: *you are being well-accepted.*
Kettledrum: *big worries ahead.*
Key, finding: *being lucky in avoiding an embarrassment.*
Key, losing: *annoyance, dispute.*
Key, using: *being under suspicion.*
Keychain-holder: *family life brings lots of joy.*
Killed, being yourself: *fear and hardship.*
King or queen, seeing or talking to: *forthcoming honor; good business deals; achieving wealth.*
Kissing a married person: *bad omen; misfortune and disagreements.*
Kissing a man, or seeing a man kissing: *unexpected desertion by your friends.*
Kissing nice girls: *true, loyal good friends.*
Kissing somebody's hand: *happiness and cheerfulness.*
Kissing, you want to: *grief and depression.*
Kitchen, and cooking: *gossip.*
Kitchen, seeing: *defamation.*
Knee, seeing damaged: *poverty, declining business.*
Knee, laying on it: *humiliation.*
Knee, swollen: *illness, exertion, losses.*
Knife, with a nice handle: *receiving gifts very soon.*
Knife, seeing or holding: *persecution, disgrace, poverty; failing business.*
Knight, seeing: *winning over a truthful friend.*
Knitting: *diligence and perseverance make your plans succeed.*
Knitted things, seeing: *bad omen, being fooled.*
Knot, seeing: *embarrassment.*
Knot, making one: *causing others embarrassment.*
Knot, undoing: *confusions clarifying, setting straight.*

L

Labyrinth, seeing: *removal of all obstacles.*
Labyrinth, walking through: *discovering secrets.*

Laboratory: *serious illness.*
Lackey, a bellman: *unexpected great joy.*
Ladder, seeing or using: *improvement of a situation; wealth and honor; happy marriage.*
Ladder, using, placing: *being robbed.*
Lady's maid: *laziness is dangerous.*
Laying out, offering things: *good, for the poor.*
Lamb, seeing hopping: *enjoying children.*
Lamp, seeing: *passing on information.*
Lamp, turning off the light: *destroying other's good prospects.*
Lance, seeing or carrying: *disagreements, efforts in vain.*
Landscape, scenery: *a pleasant, fun trip.*
Land, bare, deserted: *misfortune; annoyance; depression.*
Land, beautiful, seeing: *getting a good wife.*
Land, big and wide: *joy, amusement, fun, riches.*
Land, strange and unknown: *loss of money, bad luck.*
Land, prepared, lots of fruits: *good harvest, succeeding in your ventures.*
Lantern, burning: *secrets are being revealed.*
Lap, sitting on one: *means fondness.*
Lard, seeing: *forthcoming difficulties.*
Lark, bird, seeing: *rapid rise; success.*
Larkspur, flower: *rescued from danger*
Last will, testament, drafting: *misfortune and dissatisfaction.*
Last will, testament, from someone else: *advantage and unexpected joy.*
Lattice, fence, facing: *liberation, inner peace.*
Laughter, hearing: *experiencing sudden joy.*
Lavatory - toilet: *annoyance, boredom.*
Law, a claim defending: *receiving recognition.*
Lawyers, dealing with: *means sorrow.*
Lawsuit: *loyal friends.*
Lawn, seeing or sitting on: *adventurous life.*
Lead, being burned by: *falling into temptation.*
Lead bullets, loading: *bad conscience.*
Lead, melting: *hard working days ahead.*

Lead, seeing: *wrongful prosecution.*
Leaves, dry, withered: *interference in your plans.*
Leaves, falling: *becoming dangerously ill.*
Leaves in green, seeing: *pleasantness, experiencing.*
Learning, study: *effort and endurance will overcome all difficulties.*
Leather: *complicated business ventures.*
Leech, seeing: *self-interest, profiteering.*
Lecture, giving or hearing: *your efforts are being rewarded.*
Leg, artificial limb: *enduring bad changes.*
Leg, having a swollen or ill one: *betrayed by friends; loosing a beloved one.*
Leg, seeing being amputated: *losing a good friend.*
Leg, seeing hurt: *misfortune.*
Leg, seeing a strong one, or your own: *happiness, joy and success.*
Lemon, eating or seeing: *peace of mind, being happy.*
Lemon, squeezing: *abusiveness.*
Lemonade, drinking: *invitation to a dinner party.*
Lentil, eating: *separation and annoyance.*
Lentil, dispersing: *harming yourself.*
Lentil, seeing: *quarrel.*
Lepers, keeping company with: *experiencing unpleasantness.*
Lepers, seeing: *worries and struggle.*
Leprosy, having: *promised great wealth, success in business.*
Letter, receiving: *wealth forthcoming.*
Letter-case, seeing or finding: *resolving hidden matters.*
Letters, burning: *irresponsible blows, tricks.*
Letters, important, receiving: *whatever you have started, continues in a good way.*
Letters, not yours, opening: *annoyance.*
Letters, reading: *enjoying trust.*
Letters, sealing: *keeping secrets.*
Letters, seeing, to be read: *request for caution.*
Letters, tearing, or torn: *ugly slander; giving up a good friend.*
Letters, writing: *inconstant outlooks, unreliability.*
Lettuce, greens, eating: *good prospect.*
Lettuce, sowing, planting: *starting useless things.*

Library, seeing or own: *finding good advice.*
Lice, seeing or having: *receiving money.*
Lice, killing: *avoiding an ugly persecution.*
Life, losing your own: *unsuccessful business.*
Light, bright, burning: *health and prosperity, a soon engagement.*
Light, carrying, blown out by wind: *sudden death.*
Light, fading, seeing: *joyful trip ahead.*
Light of any kind, seeing extinguished: *forthcoming bad luck; losing a fight; disagreements.*
Light or torch, extinguished: *sadness; sickness; poverty.*
Lightening, seeing: *argument, disagreement, annoyance.*
Lilies, seeing: *power and wealth.*
Lilac tree: *illness and worries.*
Limb, losing a section of: *relief from something bad.*
Limbs, deformed, seeing: *scare ahead.*
Limousine, car seeing: *a pleasant future.*
Limp, walk with: *your good reputation is in jeopardy.*
Limp, seeing someone else: *ignorance enduring.*
Linden tree: *fulfillment of your wishes.*
Linen, fine quality: *enjoying happy days.*
Linen, trading: *prosperous business.*
Linnet, bird, seeing or hearing: *joy; good news from faraway relatives or friends.*
Lion, seeing: *gaining wealth; respect from a superior; marrying a well-educated, rich lady.*
Lion, locked up: *fear and difficulty.*
Lion killing: *overcoming your enemy.*
Lions pursuing you: *being deserted.*
Lion with cubs, seeing: *coming into danger.*
Lips, beautiful, red, having or seeing: *prosperity and health for distant friends or relatives.*
Liquors: *avoid flatterers.*
Little, being: *exalt in your status.*
Liver, eating: *steady health.*
Liver, cutting: *destroying your own health.*
Liver, seeing: *having good, nutritious food.*

Livery, Livree, official robe: *for servants - good;* **for masters** *- disadvantage.*
Livestock, a herd, seeing: *prosperity.*
Livestock, put to pasture: *disgrace, annoyance.*
Lizard, seeing: *big chances in business.*
Load, carrying: *finishing fast, business matters.*
Loam - pit: *you are being followed, stalked.*
Lock (pick), seeing: *being robbed.*
Locksmith: *finding out about a secret.*
Locked up: *loss of happiness.*
Logging, wood: *means death.*
Locomotive: *daydreamer - your head is in the clouds.*
Lost, your belongings: *judge your own opinions, and you will be well off.*
Lottery draw: *big losses.*
Lotto, playing: *cozy company enjoying.*
Lover, seeing or being alone together: *temptation.*
Luck, or sudden wealth: *pursued by friends, harassed by creditors.*
Lunar eclipse: *losing your girlfriend.*
Lute, playing: *pleasant company.*
Lye, drinking or seeing: *repulsiveness.*
Lynx, seeing: *discovering a person's cleverness.*

M

Magic: *beware of swindlers.*
Magnet, seeing or having: *experiencing popularity.*
Magpie - bird, seeing: *cheating.*
Maid, seeing: *happiness, soon to be united.*
Makeup, using: *treason, falseness.*
Malformation, deformity, seeing: *being hurt through slander.*
Male nurse: *you are earning love and gratefulness.*
Man, with nightcap: *too much comfort is not good for you.*
Man, noble, elegant, seeing: *obnoxious people, surrounding you.*
Manure, seeing: *being dishonored through bad company*

Manure, loading: *servitude for a long time.*
Manure wagon, driving: *unpleasant work.*
Maple tree, seeing: *a comfortable life.*
Maps, seeing: *a trip lies ahead.*
Marble, seeing: *getting in and out of arguments.*
Marketplace, seeing: *difficulties and hardship.*
Marmot, seeing: *poverty and laziness.*
Marriage-settlement: *sadness.*
Marten, animal killing: *liberation from unpleasantness.*
Marten, shooting: *good business deals with strangers.*
Masquerade, dressing up: *prosperous business.*
Masquerade, seeing: *being cheated.*
Mass, attending: *inner peace.*
Mass, celebrating by yourself: *difficult and depressing work.*
Mask, a face, seeing or wearing: *warning - hypocritical friends.*
Matches, using or seeing: *riches, treasures.*
Mattress, seeing: *restlessness.*
Mattress, laying on it: *pleasant relations.*
Matron, seeing: *reaching an old age.*
Meadow, seeing: *going on a pleasant excursion.*
Meal, having: *stinginess and poverty.*
Meal, having in company: *abundance and riches.*
Measles: *many hours of enjoyment.*
Meat, feeding the dogs: *scornful treatment.*
Meat, prepared, eating: *prosperity.*
Meat, raw, bought by others: *arguments, disagreement.*
Meat, raw, seeing or buying: *supportive friends; forthcoming wealth and honor.*
Medal, seeing: *being neglected.*
Medal decoration seeing or receiving: *honor and reputation.*
Medicine, bitter taste: *repression from your enemies.*
Medicine, to see being prescribed: *continuation of illness.*
Medicine, giving to others: *advantage and benefit.*
Medicine, discharged by intestines: *good business deals.*
Medicine, herb roots, seeing or eating: *end of annoying business.*
Medicine, seeing: *indisposition.*

Medicine, spitting out: *bad luck, trouble in your business transaction.*
Medicine, taking: *repulsiveness.*
Medicine, using: *loosing money.*
Meeting a friend: *good omen.*
Meeting with an enemy: *bad omen.*
Melons, seeing or eating: *stability in your marriage; but he is an unsatisfying entertainer.*
Merry-go-round, riding on or seeing: *coming into entanglements.*
Merchandise, buying or selling: *activity brings huge profit.*
Mercury: *unsteady, restless life.*
Mermaid, seeing: *treason or prosecution.*
Meteorological observation: *pursued by false friends.*
Mice, seeing or catching: *successful business; good marriage and prosperity.*
Mice, hear them squeak: *entering a period of grief.*
Microscope, looking through: *try to improve your flaws.*
Midwife, seeing or talking (? to): *happiness; a secret goes public.*
Milk, drinking: *your occupation advances through economics.*
Milk, buying: *success in all sort of things.*
Milk truck/wagon: *going on a nice trip.*
Mill, seeing in operation: *to be happy and rich.*
Mill stone, seeing: *growing family.*
Mill- wheel, getting caught in: *coming into great danger.*
Millet, eating: *a family life and big estate.*
Milt, our organ, seeing: *festivities and fun.*
Mine, seeing: *growth –in wealth and property.*
Miner, pitman seeing: *unwanted visitor.*
Mirror, breaking: *hostility.*
Mirror, seeing: *for healthy people -* *joy / honor;* *for ill people -* *death.*
Mirror, seeing yourself in: *being betrayed.*
Mirror, with a golden frame: *coming into a better status through extraordinary circumstances.*
Miserable, feeling: *worrisome days.*
Misery, a big one, seeing: *contempt.*
Mist - fog, covering the sun: *eye illness.*
Mist - fog, disappearing: *being cleared of false accusations.*

Mist - fog, dense: *encounter complex matters.*
Mite, maggot, seeing: *dispute at home.*
Molasses: *tricks been used to get you.*
Mole, seeing: *injury, harm.*
Monastery, seeing: *peace and a happy old age.*
Money, copper: *effortless work.*
Money, counting: *happiness, great fortune.*
Money exchange, stock trading: *lots of luck.*
Money, finding: *profit, gain, good prospect for the future.*
Money, full bags of: *a secure, pleasant future.*
Money, losing: *embarrassment, bad circumstances.*
Money- coins, finding: *becoming happy.*
Money- coins, paying with: *increase in respect.*
Money- coins, receiving: *getting along well; joy.*
Money- coins, seeing: *joyfulness; profit.*
Money, paying with: *freeing yourself from a burden.*
Money, receiving: *nervousness, being restless.*
Money, seeing: *falling into temptation.*
Money, a full wallet: *good progress in ventures.*
Money, wallet, empty: *sustaining losses.*
Monk, seeing: *being in good company.*
Monks, talking to: *reconciliation, coming to terms with your offenders.*
Monkey, killing: *overcome your enemy.*
Monkey, seeing: *being cheated by flatterers.*
Monkeys, seeing them bite (fleas): *illness;* **for people who are in love**
  - their wishes will come true.
Monkeys, seeing dancing: *a lot of amusement and fun.*
Monster, seeing: *great misfortune; annoyance; false hopes.*
Monument, seeing: *sickness.*
Moon, bright shining: *sincere joy, being truly loved.*
Moon, seeing its first quarter: *succeeding in love and trade.*
Moon, seeing in the water (reflection): *pleasant acquaintance.*
Moon, seeing decline: *fading love, damage in business trading.*
Moor- land, dry, seeing: *your hopes are being shattered.*
Moor- land, green, seeing: *the last beam of hope.*
Morgue, visiting or seeing: *deadly peril, losing a friend.*

Mortar: *great festivity, pleasant visitors.*
Moss: *coming into much money.*
Mosquito: *bad company will bring you down.*
Mother, seeing or talking to: *seeing a long lost friend again.*
Mountain, climbing: *effort, unpleasantness.*
Mountain, climbing, not reaching the top: *decline in ventures.*
Mountain, collapsing: *being followed by a powerful enemy.*
Mountain, descending: *small but solid profit.*
Mountains, seeing with green trees: *great hope for the future.*
Mountains, seeing with beautiful castles: *means steadfastness.*
Mountains with ruins: *interruptions in your plans.*
Mouse trap: *beware of persecution.*
Mouth, can't open: *deadly peril.*
Mussels, seeing: *bad news from afar; embarrassment that takes great effort to eliminate.*
Mustache: *idle, transient joy.*
Mustard, coarse, eating or seeing: *a bad omen.*
Mouth, huge, seeing: *respected honor, highly regarded.*
Mouth organ, (harmonica) playing or seeing: *good news.*
Mower, seen at work: *luck and blessings in business.*
Mower, seeing not in use: *losing friends.*
Moveable goods, selling: *getting involved in lawsuits.*
Muddy, dirty cloth, wearing: *misfortune and grief.*
Mud, sludge, walking through: *difficult times ahead.*
Muffs, wearing or seeing: *terrible times ahead.*
Mule, seeing or riding: *being deceived and fooled by others.*
Mulberry tree: *wealth; blessed years ahead.*
Mulberries, eating or seeing: *late, but a happy marriage.*
Murder, being of yourself: *fright, shock experiencing.*
Mushrooms: *falseness brings great disadvantages.*
Mushrooms, eating or seeing: *reaching an old age.*
Music, hear beautiful one : *receiving good, merry news.*
Mustard, fine, smooth, seeing: *suffering from gossips.*
Myrtle tree: *happily in love, enjoying respect, marrying a nice girl.*
Myrtle, seeing or wearing: *soon to be married.*

N

Nails, finding: *luck, happiness.*
Naked, yourself being: *ridicule, lots to endure.*
Naked, seeing others: *luck and bright days ahead.*
Navel, seeing: *increasing your wealth.*
Neck, a big and huge one: *happiness.*
Neck, seeing small and thin: *misfortune.*
Neck / throat, being choked by a person: *that same person will influence you.*
Neck / throat, seeing: *good omen.*
Neck / throat, swollen: *happiness.*
Necklace, neck ribbon, seeing: *honor and happiness.*
Necklace, wearing: *to be privileged, highly regarded.*
Necktie, taking off: *being protected against a cold.*
Needful, being in need: *forthcoming bad luck.*
Needles, seeing or using: *arguments.*
Negro, seeing: *disaster in undertakings.*
Neighbor, seeing or talking to: *coming into danger.*
Nets, seeing: *corruption will bring harm.*
Nettle: *libel, pursuit.*
Nest, empty, seeing: *a happy marriage.*
Nest, full, seeing: *additions to the family.*
Night–birds: *never start anything before thinking it over twice.*
Nightingale, seeing or hearing sing: *joyful news in your engagement time, happy marriage.*
Night owl, flying: *chaos between your loved ones.*
Night owl, on top of house, and crying: *a bad omen.*
Night- watchman: *thieves, causing harm.*
Nose, big, your own: *obtaining wealth and honor.*
Nose, bleeding: *enduring ignorance.*
Nose, short: *modest circumstances; happy, peaceful family life.*
Nose, clogged: *an influential man is leaving you; deceitful loyalty and friendship.*
Noise, turmoil: *nervousness and restlessness in the house.*
Northern lights, seeing: *your nicest dreams and hopes come true.*

Notary, consulting: *soon to be married.*
Notary, seeing him or her write: *being mentioned in an inheritance.*
Numbers, seeing: *through stupidity, you will lose a lot.*
Numbers, picking those you favor in a draw: *good prospect of big earnings.*
Numbers, writing: *a lot of activity and things to do.*
Numbers, seeing: *under 90 - uncertainty; over 90 - luck and prosperity.*
Numbers, not remembering: *merry, fun social gatherings.*
Numbness, freeze: *work, in vain.*
Nun, seeing or talking to: *entering a different social status.*
Nuts, eating or seeing: *wealth, happiness and honor.*
Nuts, playing with: *arguments.*
Nuts, walnuts, seeing: *annoyance; misfortune.*

O

Oak tree, a beautiful, seeing: *advantage; wealth; long life.*
Oak tree, dried out: *death of a relative or friend.*
Oath, to take or see being taken: *involvement in lawsuits.*
Obelisk, seeing: *surprised by extraordinary events.*
Ocean, or big sea, crossing: *means, disaster.*
Ocean: *(see, under "Sea")*
Ocean birds, seeing: *for travelers on sea, danger.*
Offence, being offended: *favors and kindness.*
Office, being there: *great losses, your debtor lets you down.*
Oil, beating in a mixer: *contestation.*
Oil, burning: *much effort in vain.*
Oil, being poured over you: *advantage.*
Oil, tasting a good one: *strong health.*
Oil, seeing spilled: *tremendous losses.*
Oil, saving, scooping up: *luck and advantage.*
Ointment, making: *sickness.*
Old, seeing yourself: *liberty, freedom.*
Old, becoming: *evil, it is bad.*
Olives: *temptations, hasty behavior.*

Onions, cooking: *poorness; being bothered by authorities.*
Onions, eating: *mourning, and grief.*
Onions, seeing: *secrets are being revealed.*
Opera - glass, seeing: *news to be told.*
Opponent, meeting with him: *misfortune.*
Oranges, eating or seeing: *lingering indisposition, nausea.*
Oranges, bitter tasting: *loss of honor; wealth; being misjudged.*
Orchard, walking through: *becoming rich due to inheritance; happy marriage; many good children; true love; influential friends.*
Organ, seeing or hearing being played: *joy; inheritance.*
Ornament - jewelry, seeing: *vanity creates heartbreak.*
Ostrich: *making a fuss about nothing.*
Otter - catching fish: *luck in business.*
Overcoat, seeing: *meeting great dignitaries.*
Owls, crying: *vexation, annoyance.*
Owls, seeing: *discontentedness; illness; poverty.*
Ox, seeing at work: *servitude; bondage.*
Ox, seeing: *advantage in trade affairs.*
Ox, seeing jump: *coming into danger.*
Oysters, eating /seeing: *success in your work, happy pregnancy.*

P

Pail or water bucket, seeing: *comfort.*
Pain, feeling: *hardship, luckily overcoming trouble.*
Painting, seeing a portrait of yourself: *a long life.*
Painting something in white: *pursuit, persecution.*
Painting something in black: *illness.*
Painting something in red: *joy.*
Painting, seeing: *being tempt by false friends; danger; deceived by lover; loss of a friend.*
Palace, seeing: *arrogance brings you down.*
Palisade, conquering or destroying: *security; glory; happiness.*
Palisade, seeing: *embarrassment; restlessness.*

Palm branches, seeing, carry, or collecting: *abundance, wealth; luck in business.*
Panther, seeing: *being frightened.*
Pantry, seeing: *sickness and bad luck.*
Paper, cutting: *worries about the future.*
Paper, printed-paper, seeing: *inspiring trust.*
Paper, tearing apart: *coming into anger.*
Paper, writing on: *suing and defamation.*
Parade, seeing: *the thirst for pleasure brings big disadvantage.*
Paradise, being in it: *being connected with a loving item.*
Paralyzed, being: *misery, hardship.*
Parcel- carrier, seeing: *effort and work assures a healthy spirit.*
Parchment: *an unexpected inheritance brings joy.*
Parents, arguing with them: *a bad omen.*
Parents, seeing or talking: *good fortune in ventures; cheerfulness*
Parents, siblings deceased, seeing: *confusion; bad luck.*
Park, seeing: *a comfortable life.*
Parrot, seeing: *discovering secrets.*
Parrot, is talking: *disgusting gossip.*
Party, attending, a social gathering: *life is in danger.*
Partridge, seeing: *lustful desires.*
Pass, mountain-road: hard, troublesome work.
Passport, seeing: *going on a big trip.*
Pasture, land, seeing: *danger and difficulty.*
Path, walking on a wide one: *happiness.*
Path, walking on a narrow one: *grief and annoyance.*
Pavement, seeing: *bad omen in every way.*
Pawn shop: *recklessness leads to losses.*
Pawn shop, enter: *bad business.*
Peaches, breaking in half: *coming into your desired lifestyle.*
Peaches, seeing or eating: *reunion with your estranged lover.*
Peacock, seeing: *rapid progress in ventures; lucky connections; many courtesies on a trip.*
Pearl, seeing or own: *misfortune, discomfort.*
Pearls, sorting them: *lonely, boring life.*
Pear tree, shaking: *intemperance.*

Pears, beautiful, hanging on a tree: *good prospect for the future.*
Pears, being eaten by insects: *insidiousness.*
Pears, good ones, seeing or eating: *overcoming disagreements.*
Pears, sour, eating: *annoyance in your household.*
Peas, eating: *luck in ventures.*
Peas, planting: *hope, succeeding in your plans.*
Peas, seeing or picking: *prosperity; growing wealth; cheerfulness.*
Peas, growing, seen in bloom: *good progress in your deeds.*
Pencils: *receiving a good message.*
Penitentiary: *rescue from imminent danger.*
Pennant, seeing: *people of authority favor you.*
Penny, seeing: *charity brings reward.*
People, walking towards you: *sadness, affliction.*
People, dressed in black: *coming into danger of death.*
People, seeing many: *bad luck, disaster.*
People, old ones, seeing: *luck, lots of blessings.*
Pepper, seeing or using: *being offended.*
Pursuing something: *unpleasantness.*
Petrel, storm-birds: *risky wanderings.*
Petticoat, colorful, seeing: *doubtful success in love; or otherwise in business.*
Petticoat, white, seeing: *a rare enjoyment.*
Pharmacy, seeing, being in it: *coming in contact with profiteers and evil people.*
Piano, playing or seeing: *dispute; conflict between friends.*
Pictures, beautiful, seeing: *being cheated.*
Pictures, big, bad looking ones: *finding friends, being happy.*
Pies, pastries seeing: *excessiveness leads to illness.*
Pigs, seeing: *deceived by servants, removing unpleasantness.*
Pig, rolling in the mud: *getting an evil housekeeper.*
Pig-shed: *disadvantaged business.*
Pike, seeing: *coming into danger.*
Pills, tablets, seeing: *beware of folly and fools.*
Pilgrim seeing: *news from abroad.*
Pilgrimage: *your start is commendable.*
Pillar, seeing: *means honor.*

Pillar, collapsing: *invalidism, illness.*
Pin cushion, needles: *a nice gift will surprise you.*
Pin, seeing or having: *getting lots of rewarding work.*
Pineapple, eating: *being invited as a guest.*
Pipe, seeing: *pleasant circumstances.*
Pistol: *pursuit by enemies.*
Pit, seeing or falling into: *sudden misfortune, being tricked.*
Pit, climbing out with great effort: *pursuit; having friends unknown to yourself.*
Pit, getting out with ease: *managing many big difficulties.*
Place, seeing: *friendly reception.*
Plains, seeing: *happiness and enjoyment.*
Planting: *prosperity; authority; prestige.*
Plaster-ornaments: *disaster in your plans.*
Plaster, white wash: *huge expenses are ahead.*
Pliers, seeing or having: *treason or pursuit.*
Plow, seeing, or your own: *soon to be happily married.*
Plow, destroying: *interruption in your trade, job.*
Plowing: *good progress in business.*
Plums, eating or seeing: *bad times ahead.*
Plums, oval, freestone, eating: *shock, sickness.*
Plums, Italian, freestone, hanging on trees: *prosperous future.*
Poison, giving somebody: *disagreement, annoyance.*
Poison, taking and dying: *giving bad advice.*
Polecat, seeing: *miserable sickness.*
Poles, sticks: *disagreements.*
Police: *repulsiveness, disagreements ahead.*
Pomegranates, seeing: *coming into wealth through a last will or luck.*
Pond, seeing a little one: *getting a beautiful woman; wishes come true; joy from your family.*
Pope, seeing or talking to: *happiness, cheerfulness.*
Poplar, whisper or seeing: *a good outcome from a project.*
Poppy-seed head, seeing: *becoming ill.*
Porcupine: *warning about mockery and envy.*
Pork meat: *to remain in an ordinary social class.*
Portraying yourself: *long life.*

Portraying, by a painter: *having good friends.*
Portrait, seeing: *long life for the person you are seen.*
Portrait, your own, giving away: *treason; betrayal; disagreement.*
Portrait, of a beautiful girl: *soon to be married.*
Portrait, carrying and breaking: *imminent disaster.*
Portrait, seeing being painted: *abide in your love.*
Portrait, receiving as a gift: *lots of fun ahead.*
Post / stake, pushing into the ground: *effortless work.*
Post, mail delivery car: *pleasant news.*
Potatoes, digging out: *effort, getting little thanks for hard work.*
Potatoes, eating or seeing: *becoming sick.*
Pots, seeing: *gain in wealth.*
Pots, breaking: *a fun party.*
Poultry, feeding: *soon to be engaged.*
Praying: *joy and peace of mind.*
Prayer book: *comfort in your sorrow.*
Preaching: *a moderate lifestyle keeps your health.*
Pregnant woman, seeing: *unpleasantness lies ahead.*
Pregnant woman, making fun of: *being freed of worries.*
Priest, standing in pulpit: *experiencing repulsiveness.*
Prison, being released from: *illness; or death.*
Prison building, seeing: *inner peace.*
Prison, being escorted into: *happiness and well-being.*
Prison, living in it: *comforted by friends.*
Procession, attending or seeing: *happiness and joy.*
Profit, receiving: *arrival of a friend.*
Profiteer, talking or doing business: *illegal business temptations.*
Profiteering: *shame, loss of fortune.*
Property, nice estate, an inheritance gift: *a happy and profitable marriage.*
Prostitute, seeing or talking to: *happy days and luck.*
Protection, finding: *misery, ramification.*
Protractor, seeing: *you will commence construction.*
Provoke: *hostility, discord.*
Pub / Inn, lodging: *calmness by disagreements and complaints.*
Pub, or saloon, seeing: *getting some rest.*

Public festival, attending: *unstable luck, personal mishap.*
Puddle / Dog: *corrupt company gives you a bad reputation.*
Pulpit, standing in it, or seeing: *being honored in public.*
Pump in action: *surprises, very good omen.*
Pump - well, empty or dry: *poverty; misfortune, bad luck.*
Pumpkin, eating: *sickness.*
Pumpkin, playing with: *separation from a favored thing.*
Pumpkins, seeing hanging: *having many mentors.*
Puppet show, seeing: *getting a subordinate job.*
Puppet: *loyal, devoted servants.*
Purchasing, something: *extravagance, waste, brings disadvantage.*
Purgatory: *be careful not to sin.*
Purse, wallet, an empty one: *sustaining losses.*
Purse, wallet with money: *advancing business transactions.*
Pyramids climbing: *good business.*
Pyramids seeing: *happiness and honor.*

Q

Quail-bird, seeing, hearing: *dispute; treason; disagreements; bad luck in marriage.*
Quarrel: *unexpected news.*
Quackery: *stupidity brings harm.*
Quince - fruit, seeing, or having: *happiness in marriage, wealth, peace of mind.*

R

Rabbi: *being in pleasant company soon.*
Rabbit, seeing: *being fearful, fear of death.*
Rabbit meat, eating: *peace of mind..*
Rabbit, shooting: *being happy.*
Radish: *simple nutrition keeps you healthy.*
Rage, getting into: *an overdue business matter comes to an end.*
Rain, seeing or being in it: *happy family life, steadiness love.*

Rain, thunder, lightning, getting wet: *discord, and bad luck.*
Rainbow, seeing: *lots of efforts in vain, troublesome luck.*
Raisins: *excessiveness leads to ruin.*
Rake, seeing: *expect some news.*
Ram, being kicked or pushed by: *pursuit.*
Ram, seeing: *profit.*
Ranger, meeting: *imminent mischief, unpleasantness.*
Raped, being: *disaster in every way.*
Raped, publicly: *disaster and declining enterprises or ventures.*
Rasp: *a lot of uproar for nothing.*
Raspberries, eating / seeing: *enjoyment, pleasures awaiting you.*
Rats, catching: *to settle a dispute.*
Rats, seeing: *many enemies; deceived by friends.*
Ravens claws, seeing: *disaster; disagreements.*
Raven, flying around you: *death.*
Reading: *receiving good news.*
Reaper, grain, in a field: *luck in business.*
Receipt: *losses ahead.*
Reed - plant, seeing in water: *indecision brings drawbacks and disadvantage.*
Relatives, seeing or talking to: *delusion, fraud.*
Relic, seeing: *danger of losing money and estate.*
Resting, relaxing: *danger ahead.*
Respect, showing: *humiliation.*
Respect, receiving: *favorable establishments.*
Restaurant / Inn: *great unrest lies ahead.*
Restaurant, serving meals: *creating hatred and envy.*
Resurrection of the dead: *rescue from misery.*
Retailing - sales: *treason, pursuit.*
Revenge: *long-lasting involvement in a lawsuit.*
Review of troops: *imprisonment.*
Ribs, seeing: *happiness in the family, luck in business.*
Rice, eating or seeing: *plenty of money and assets are forthcoming.*
Rich, being: *in danger of losing everything.*
Rich people, seeing / talking, getting along well: *receiving good deeds and rewards.*

Rifle, going hunting: *unfaithfulness.*
Rifle, seeing a nice looking one: *falling in love.*
Rifle, and shooting: *big embarrassment.*
Ring, hammer around a barrel: *new connections.*
Ring of gold and precious stones: *coming into well-off circumstances.*
Ring, finding: *happiness lies ahead.*
Ring, giving as a present: *becoming a bride or groom.*
Ring, losing: *unexpected separation from a lover; friend or relative.*
Rivalry: *unsuccessful ventures.*
River, crossing over: *overcome dangerous enemies.*
River, crashing over rocks: *a family member faces ruin.*
River, falling into: *misfortune.*
River, overflowing: *stop, project is being hindered.*
River, being swept downstream: *annoyance; danger; persecution.*
River, roaring: *slander, blasphemy.*
Roaring, howling of animals: *bad news.*
Roast beef, eating or seeing: *profitable, good business.*
Roast, smelling: *running errands unnecessary.*
Robber, being killed by: *losing your inheritance.*
Robber, seeing, being held up: *casual ties with relatives; and children or fortunes.*
Rock, ascending easily: *reaching your goals.*
Rock climbing: *conquest.*
Rock, climbing and not reaching the top: *stand still, decline in business.*
Rock, descending from easily: *losing friends or relatives.*
Rock, a tall one seeing: *undertaking a enormous project.*
Rocks, seeing: *work and effort.*
Rocket, seeing rising: *changeable luck; unsteady love; invitation to a happy party.*
Rod, someone hitting: *advantage, overpowering.*
Royalty, seen on horseback or in a carriage: *leaning towards wastefulness.*
Royalty, seeing: *honor.*
Royalty, talking to: *being envied.*
Roof, full of swallows: *going on a trip.*

Roof, eaves, standing under: *unpleasantness, difficulty.*
Roof, falling down from: *unpleasant news.*
Roof, seeing on a house: *domesticity.*
Room, sweeping: *effort and tenacity leads to your goals.*
Rooms, nicely wallpapered: *flourishing trade.*
Rope, being made: *declining prosperity.*
Rope, being tied up with: *good fortune and honor.*
Rope, cutting: *harming others.*
Rope, climbing down on: *danger in your activities.*
Rope, tightrope walker: *a risky venture brings harm.*
Rooster, crowing: *caution.*
Rooster, seeing: *being liked by women.*
Roosters, fighting: *difficulties in marriage.*
Rosebuds, seeing: *discovery of a precious object.*
Rosebush with many roses: *family addition.*
Roses, seeing faded: *vexation, unsteady love, bad luck.*
Roses, in full bloom: *blessings and happiness.*
Rosemary, seeing: *you will earn a good reputation.*
Rosehip, eating: *poverty.*
Roots: *secure living standard, being well-off.*
Rowing: *having hard, but rewarding work.*
Ruins, seeing: *sloppiness brings harm.*
Rum, drinking: *excessiveness is health damaging.*
Running, and not moving ahead: *much effort in vain.*
Running, or seeing someone run: *fulfillment of your wishes; being lucky.*

S

Saber: *perseverance leads you towards your goal.*
Sack, bag, heavy, carrying: *harmful times.*
Sacks, full, seeing: *abundance in all earthly things.*
Sack, being carried: *lots of expenses.*
Sack, seeing with holes: *losses.*
Sacks, many piled on a wagon: *flourishing trade.*

Sad, being: *making new friends.*
Sad, being, not knowing why: *very bad omen.*
Sailor, seeing or talking to: *misfortune on trips.*
Sailor, arriving on a ship: *news from a friend or relative afar.*
Sailboat: *a big trip ahead.*
Saint, worship: *blessings at your work.*
Salad: *a time of tests lies ahead.*
Saliva and vomiting: *excessiveness ruins your health.*
Salmon, eating: *you will make a find.*
Salt, scatter: *annoyance.*
Sand, seeing: *insecurity in everything.*
Sausage, eating: *unexpected visitor, flirtation.*
Sausage, seeing or making: *struggle.*
Saw, seeing your own: *a business deal is happily finalized.*
Saw-blade, seeing or using: *good progress in your business.*
Scabs, scabies: *fear and worries unnecessary.*
Scaffold, seeing: *be on guard.*
Scale, seeing: *you will make good business deals.*
Scandal, experiencing: *disagreements; hostility.*
Scared, being: *grief and food shortages.*
Scarecrow, seeing: *having dishonest friends.*
Scars, getting or having: *glory and honor.*
Scepter: *a demanding behavior is always disliked.*
School, attending: *means happiness.*
School, schoolchildren, seeing: *being cheated, and sorrow.*
Schoolteacher: *difficult and troublesome business.*
Scissors, using: *involvement in unpleasantness.*
Scissors, seeing: *gain, profit.*
Scorpion, seeing: *careful, malicious enemies.*
Scuffle, a fight: *don't get involved in the affairs of others.*
Scythe, to own or see: *being offended by friends.*
Scythe, mowing or seeing: *shows gain, profit; getting hard working servants.*
Sea, calm and cruising: *happy union, coming into great riches.*
Sea, cruising, landing on a deserted place: *with effort and difficulty reaching your goal at last, reward through success.*

Sea, stormy, cruising on: *lots of complaints in love or business.*
Seal, seeing: *joyfulness.*
Seal-signet ring, using: *coming out of threatening danger; enjoying security.*
Sealing letters: *many business deals.*
Seats, stools, seeing: *distinction, honor.*
Secluded place, being there: *illness and danger.*
Seeds, picked by birds: *losing confidence.*
Seeds, selling: *making good business deals.*
Seeds, sorting: *means good progress in business.*
Seeing your deceased relatives and friends: *grief and sorrow.*
Seminar, attending: *betrayal, or being fooled.*
Sentenced, seeing people: *losing some of your friends.*
Sentry box, seeing: *being safe from enemies.*
Seraglio - harem: *exuberance is the ruin of the soul and body.*
Sewing kit: *increase of your income.*
Sewing, stitching: *your work comes in very handy.*
Shadow, walking in it: *leaving an oppressing relationship.*
Sheaf, tying together: *new acquaintance.*
Sheaf, loading, harvesting: *efforts are being rewarded.*
Sheaf's, seeing: *humiliation from your enemies.*
Sheaf's, lots of spikes, seeing: *good fortune.*
Sheep, grazing: *health and happiness.*
Sheep, pushing each other: *sufferings.*
Shepherd, seeing: *caution in ventures.*
Shepherd, seeing with a herd: *gaining wealth.*
Shelter, from rain: *hidden annoyance.*
Shelter, seeking from enemies: *fraud.*
Ship, building: *grandiose, giant projects.*
Ship, burning: *huge losses.*
Ship, fighting the waves: *lots of conflict with your enemies.*
Ship, in harbor: *no changes in your tasks.*
Ship - machinery, seeing: *unexpected news from your creditors.*
Ship, sailing under a bridge: *approaching danger; and luckily overcoming it.*
Ship, seeing or being on it: *unexpected good news.*

Ship, sinking: *frightened by sad news.*
Ship, stranded: *huge embarrassment.*
Ship, with many passengers: *emigration.*
Ship, without sail or mast: *rescue from trouble or misery.*
Shirt, taking off: *frustrated about your hopes.*
Shirt, torn, seeing: *means great success.*
Shirt, nice seeing: *forthcoming prosperity.*
Shirt, washing or ironing: *striving for affection.*
Shock, terror: *joyful news.*
Shoes, buying: *overly hasty.*
Shoes, cutting apart: *getting sore feet.*
Shoe, fitting: *making suitable undertakings, for your business.*
Shoe, new, trying on: *good omen.*
Shoe, sole, losing: *trouble, inconvenience ahead.*
Shoe, too tight, putting on: *severe depression.*
Shoemaker, seeing: *a troublesome life.*
Shooting: *through endurance, reaching your goals.*
Shopping: *advantage, gain.*
Shore, going for a walk: *coming into danger.*
Shot, hearing: *complications.*
Shotgun, shooting: *anger, false hopes of making profits.*
Shoulder, broken: *unpleasantness.*
Shoulder, deformed: *loving other women.*
Shoulders, shrug: *carrying doubtful plans.*
Shoulders, extremely high: *strength and patience.*
Shoulders, swollen: *annoyance with your loved ones.*
Shovel, seeing or using: *getting unrewarding work.*
Shroud, seeing: *long-lasting illness.*
Shrub - bush, seeing: *falling in love quickly.*
Shrub or bushes, cutting down: *seeing unpleasantness diminish.*
Shrub or bushes, getting hurt by: *losses in business.*
Shrub - bushes, walking through some distance: *obstacles of different kinds.*
Siblings, seeing deceased: *long life.*
Siblings, seeing dying: *enemies disappear.*
Sick, and being in pain: *misery and bad luck.*

Sickness, hidden suffering from: *dishonorable wealth.*
Sick people, visiting and comforting: *joy, cheer; happiness.*
Sickle, seeing or using: *profit.*
Sickle, sharpen: *pleasant message.*
Side of your body, swollen or injured: *huge wealth; happiness.*
Sieve, seeing: *an unanswered request.*
Sign, seeing: *involvement in disputes.*
Sign, pointing to an Inn: *beware of rivalry.*
Sign post: *you enter a tricky situation.*
Silk dress, wearing: *you enter a desired status in society.*
Silk dress, tearing: *a presented goodness; luck; misjudged.*
Silk, in red color: *forthcoming casualty.*
Silk, seeing or using: *flourishing business.*
Silkworm, finding or seeing: *many truthful friends.*
Silk material, woven: *hesitation in your course of business.*
Silver, seeing: *pursuit by false friends; deceived by your lover.*
Silver, dishes: *coming into good circumstances.*
Silver, in small coins: *unpleasant and losses.*
Silver, precious coins, receiving: *joy, money; and gain in real estate.*
Silver things, wearing: *servitude.*
Silver pieces, having: *unpleasantness.*
Silver pieces, selling off: *improvement in business.*
Single, being: *union.*
Singing: *you will hear uncomfortable things.*
Singing, hearing: *good news from afar from friends or relatives.*
Singing in the bathtub: *losing your voice.*
Singing in front of a sovereign: *getting a hang of criticizing.*
Singing, nice songs with a clear voice: *everyone is well and happy.*
Singing with a fun crowd: *different people's opinions to hear.*
Siskin - bird, seeing or hearing: *be steadfast in your plans.*
Sisters or brothers, seeing or talking to: *annoyance, disagreements.*
Skating: *means much success.*
Skating, watching: *interruptions in your business.*
Skeleton: *shock, being frightened.*
Skeleton, from an animal: *arguments; quarrel about pedantry.*
Skeleton bones, seeing: *trouble and unpleasantness.*

Skin, eczema: *careful, danger to your health.*
Skin, dark colored or black, seeing or your own: *being cheated and deserted by friends or relatives.*
Skirt, too tight, wearing: *experiencing hardship.*
Skirt, full of spots: *defamation, slander.*
Skull - cross-bones, seeing: *finding out about hidden secrets.*
Sky, clear, blue, and sunny: *lots of joy; being lucky in ventures; your partner takes you to the altar.*
Sky, cloudy, red or dark: *vexation, feud, annoyance with your superior.*
Sky, flying up to: *modest wishes are being granted.*
Sky, with lots of clouds: *unfaithfulness.*
Sky, seeing the sun: *discovering clarity in a twisted matter.*
Slap in the face: *keeping evil company.*
Slapping someone: *peace and calmness in your family, good progress in your approach to love.*
Slate seeing: *effort completes your task.*
Slaughterhouse, seeing, or being in one: *fatal projects.*
Slaves, seeing: *imprisonment.*
Sled: *fun, amusement that doesn't satisfy.*
Sleep, nightcap, hat: *indolence will bring you harm.*
Sleep, and being disturbed: *annoyance.*
Sleeping in a car: *unease and worried times experiencing.*
Sleeping in a church: *neglect of your business.*
Sleeping in a gazebo: *a promising future.*
Sleeping with an ugly person: *ill-humored; sickness.*
Sleeping with your parents: *happiness, honor, contentment.*
Sleepwalker, seeing: *becoming ill.*
Sleepwalking: *imminent accident.*
Sleeve, taking apart: *divisions.*
Sleeves, having wide ones: *acquaintance.*
Sleeves, long ones: *great honor.*
Sleeves, losing: *return where it began, starting over again.*
Slippers, worn out: *annoyance.*
Slippers, wearing, walking in: *good conscience, inner peace.*
Smallpox, having or seeing: *receiving money from unexpected circumstances.*

Smell, a good fragrance: *loyal friendship.*
Smell, a bad odor: *unfaithfulness; phony people.*
Smoke, coming through a chimney: *engagement ceremony, being present.*
Smoke, seeing: *happiness just for show, deception.*
Smuggler: *entanglement, complications.*
Snail, seeing: *good news.*
Snake, being bitten: *disturbance in a happy relationship.*
Snake, killing: *getting rid of a rival.*
Snake, seeing: *female enemy; being deceived.*
Snare, trap, seeing: *betrayal.*
Snipe - bird, eating: *sadness; acquaintance with false and ungrateful friends.*
Snipe - bird, flying: *experiencing lots of changes.*
Snow, seeing, walking through: *prospect of multiple luck, flourishing business.*
Snowballs, throwing: *injuring your body.*
Snowflakes, falling: *good promises receiving.*
Soap, using or seeing: *unclear business, sorting out; being supported by friends and relatives.*
Soap bubbles, blowing: *enjoying a brief happiness.*
Soap, having a piece: *vanity brings damage.*
Solar eclipse: *means war; and hard times ahead.*
Soldiers pursuing you: *unrest and bad luck.*
Soliciting: *difficulties and misery in the family.*
Solicitor, begging for charity: *cheerfulness.*
Solicitor, seeing: *troublesome future.*
Solicitor, entering a house: *vexation, annoyance.*
Solicitor, sending away: *misery, deficiency, often also prison.*
Solicitors, giving something: *success in ventures; returned love.*
Soot, finding in your meal: *annoyance.*
Soup: *hard consistent work, provides plenty to live on.*
Sown, seeing or doing it: *wealth, happiness and health.*
Sparks, flying around: *a tendency for extravagance.*
Sparrow, seeing lots together: *means ruin.*
Sparrow hawk, catching: *triumphant over your enemies.*

Spear, seeing: *hate and hostility.*
Spectacle, live show, seeing, attending: *happiness in marriage; success in your deeds.*
Spelling, learning: *for those who work - good; for the lazy - bad.*
Spider, seeing: *a lawsuit.*
Spiders, many: *annoyance; depression; sadness.*
Spider, killing: *losing money.*
Spider web: *someone is trying to get a secret out of you.*
Spine, broken: *losing money; friends; death of a dear relative.*
Spine, a long one: *derision, scoffing.*
Sponge, to wash yourself, using or seeing: *treason; greed.*
Sponge, burning, taking out of your pocket: *escaping from danger of fire.*
Spoon, seeing: *as a guest, being invited.*
Sprinter: *precipitance gets you in trouble.*
Spruce tree, seeing or standing under: *being fooled or tricked.*
Spurge: *confiding in a disloyal person.*
Spur - silver, wearing: *great wealth.*
Spy, seeing: *beware of inconstancy.*
Squirrel, seeing: *a good marriage for a single woman—; for a married person - worries about the children.*
Squirrel, biting you: *a bad husband, for a single person; for a married person - bad children.*
Stab, being stabbed: *fear and danger.*
Stable, being in: *bondage.*
Stable, with nice livestock: *prosperity.*
Stag - deer, seeing: *gain, profit.*
Stairs, seeing: *joy; advantage.*
Stairs, walking down: *obtaining treasures.*
Stairs, walking up: *sorrow, sadness.*
Stake, a post: *defiance.*
Stalk, being stalked: *dangerous intentions.*
Starlings: *pleasant, joyful news.*
Stars, seeing in the sky: *luck in love; joyful news from friends or relatives.*
Stars, or shooting stars: *unexpected happiness awaits you.*

Statue, seeing: *embarrassment.*
Statue, tipping over: *a departure.*
Steam engine, seeing: *great wealth.*
Steam ship, traveling on: *bringing an affair, or matter quickly to an end.*
Stealing, from you: *loss of friends.*
Stick seeing: *coming under a strict leadership.*
Stirrup, seeing: *going on a trip soon.*
Stock, inventory taking: *receiving an inheritance.*
Stockings, of silk, putting on: *poverty.*
Stockings, of cotton or linen: *luck, proves to be changeable.*
Stockings, pulling down: *returning happiness.*
Stockings, with holes: *happiness for show, pretending.*
Stomach, seeing: *casualties.*
Stone, precious, seeing: *falling into temptation.*
Stone, precious, own: *great honor.*
Stone, precious, receiving: *increasing wealth.*
Stone, precious, wearing: *arrogance.*
Stone chisel: *reward for deeds well done.*
Stone, cutting in a quarry: *obtaining property, real estate.*
Stones, walking over: *struggle and suffering.*
Stool - human feces, seeing: *riches, great wealth.*
Stool - human feces, stepping into: *an unexpected, large fortune.*
Store, with lots of merchandise: *significant business.*
Stork, seeing: *happy marriage, many children turn out well.*
Storm, being in it: *bad luck in love, unfaithfulness.*
Storm and rain, experiencing: *your wishes come true.*
Storm, and trees falling: *avoiding huge disasters.*
Stove, glowing: *becoming lavish, prodigal.*
Stove, seeing: *disaster and separation.*
Stove pipe, seeing: *small losses.*
Strangers, talking, or seeing: *honor; business progress.*
Straw bundle, seeing: *prosperity.*
Straw mat: *moderation keeps you healthy.*
Straw, on fire: *luck and flourishing business.*
Straw roof, seeing: *becoming poor through misfortune.*

Straw scattered: *misery and annoyance.*
Strawberries, eating or seeing: *your children bringing you joy; a late, but good marriage; success in business; long-lasting health.*
Strawberries, seeing lots: *a growing friendship.*
Strawberries, huge, seeing: *means pride.*
Strawberries, handing out: *you will be well remembered.*
Strawberries, picking, big ones: *great joy.*
Street ballad, singing: *acquaintances bring you into difficult times.*
Street, long with nice houses: *surprised by something beautiful; friendly reception.*
Street, with many people: *you will get lots of business.*
Stretcher, seeing: *indicates death.*
Studying: *long-lasting joy.*
Stutter, stammer: *making a strong resolution.*
Suburb, seeing: *getting a small profit.*
Sugar - sweets, eating: *advantage, profit.*
Suitcase, seeing: *forthcoming trip.*
Sulfate, seeing: *abolishing false rumors, clearing your name.*
Sulfate light, strike: *imminent and serious illness.*
Sulfate handling, working with: *poor income.*
Sun, shining bright: *luck in enterprise; gaining wealth; a position in public office.*
Sun, shining into your bed: *serious illness.*
Sun, becoming dark: *a bad omen, obstacles in business.*
Sun, falling from the sky: *means death of a dignitary.*
Sun - reflection, seen in water: *empty promises.*
Sunflower: *prestige and honor.*
Sunrise, glowing red: *imminent accident.*
Sunset, beautiful seeing: *a peaceful, cheerful life.*
Sunset, glowing: *regaining your health.*
Swallow - bird, seeing: *a happy message, luck in love.*
Swallows, hearing twitter: *settlement in a started dispute.*
Swallows nesting outside your house: *being steadfast; growing harmony and happiness in your family.*
Swallows, flying in swarms: *having a large family.*
Swallow - nest: *happy family and rewarding business.*

Swamp, stepping into: *misfortune, annoyance in business.*
Swans, seeing: *happiness in marriage; many children; a long and happy life; for lovers - truthful and faithful returning love.*
Swearing, or someone else is swearing: *unpleasant news, sadness.*
Sweeping, a room: *patience in ventures, joyful success.*
Sweeping - dirt, stepping into: *trouble in your household.*
Sweets, candy, chocolates, eating: *advantage and benefit.*
Swellings, tumor, seeing or having: *wealth and riches.*
Swimming and sinking: *disaster and prosecution.*
Swimming in clear water: *luck and progress in business.*
Swimming in cloudy water: *bad omen.*
Swimming, your life is in danger: *rescue from a great danger, threat, or risk.*
Swimming, ashore: *an almost impossible dream comes true.*
Swimming and rescuing someone: *escaping a great danger.*
Sword, having one: *experiencing honor.*
Sword, nice polished, receiving: *power, controlling others.*
Sword, losing: *losing your established respect.*
Sword, breaking apart: *very bad omen.*
Sword, with soft handle, receiving as a gift: *forthcoming - great honor.*

T

Table, seeing decorated: *great joy.*
Table, setting yourself: *prosperity and wealth.*
Tail, seeing: *being insulted.*
Tailor, seeing at his job: *fraud and treason.*
Tallow - candles, making or seeing: *reaching calm; inner peace; retirement.*
Tar, seeing: *be aware of tricky companionship around you.*
Task, officially having / receiving: *enduring losses.*
Tea, drinking: *confused, muddled business.*
Teakettle: *unpleasant messages will surprise you.*
Teacher, seeing or talking to: *being cheated.*

Teeth, losing them: *losing friends through death; or otherwise unexpected misfortune.*
Teeth, cleaning: *trying hard and struggle for others.*
Telegraph - pole, seeing: *going on a distant trip.*
Tenant, seeing: *good social standing, being well-off.*
Tent, seeing: *your job is not secure.*
Testament: *(see under Last Will)*
Testimony, giving: *being favored by a distinguished, noble person.*
Theatre, seeing: *invitation to parties.*
Thermometer: *unstable friendship.*
Thieves, breaking in: *good luck; secure business deals.*
Thigh, broken, seen or having: *dying far away from your family; marrying in a foreign country.*
Thigh, having nice ones: *luck on trips and in undertakings.*
Thighs, extremely strong ones seeing: *family and honor.*
Thighs, seeing nice white ones: *health and happiness.*
Thimble, wearing: *hard work and effort are in vain.*
Thin - skinny, being yourself: *strong health.*
Thirst, cannot be quenched: *endless efforts in some matters; sadness and unrest.*
Thirst, to quench excessively: *happiness, honor; great wealth.*
Thistles, seeing: *treason; betrayal.*
Thorns, being pricked by: *withdrawing from an acquaintance.*
Thread, unwinding: *discovery of a secret.*
Thread, entangle: *secrets are well protected.*
Thread, seeing: *infatuate and charming.*
Thresh, seeing: *efforts are in vain.*
Throat, seeing: *your hopes are being fulfilled.*
Throne, seeing: *coming to honor and authority.*
Thunder, lightning, hearing or seeing: *being chased into fear.*
Thunder, lightning, no damage caused: *happy reunion with a boy- or girlfriend.*
Thunder, lightning, ignite: *experiencing losses before long.*
Thunder, without lightning: *a happy message.*
Thunder storm: *bad news.*
Tie, seeing: *vanity creates heartbreak.*

Tied-up, being: *invitation to a date; rendezvous.*
Tin, seeing: *means illness.*
Tinder: *danger ahead.*
Tinker, seeing: *arguments with your neighbors.*
Tidbit, little pieces, enjoying: *lack of moderation makes you sick.*
Toad, seeing: *losing friends, fraud, pursuit by enemies.*
Toad, killing: *triumph over your enemies.*
Tobacco box: *improving health.*
Tobacco, handing out: *annoyance.*
Tobacco, taking, inhaling: *forthcoming thirst for pleasure, sex.*
Tobacco, pipe, smoking: *means success.*
Tobacco - pipe, seeing: *arguments.*
Tobacco - pipe, breaking apart: *reconciliation with an enemy.*
Toilet, lavatory: *annoyance, boredom.*
Tongue, seeing: *enduring slander and malignity.*
Tools, seeing: *lots of rewarded work ahead.*
Toothache: *after sorrow — follows joy.*
Toothpick, using or seeing: *very bad omen.*
Toothbrush: *a screening in your social circle is necessary.*
Torch, carrying: *you are being loved.*
Torch, glowing: *shedding light on mysterious, vague matters.*
Torch, seeing falling from the sky: *headache.*
Torch, putting out: *destroying a comfortable relation.*
Torture, suffering from: *lots of distress.*
Towel, seeing: *great relief from nasty, awkward things.*
Tower, collapsing: *imminent misfortune.*
Tower bells, hearing: *you will soon hear pleasant news.*
Towers, seeing them in gold: *envy and hate.*
Tower, decorated with stone ornaments: *huge advantage.*
Toys, seeing: *stay away from childishness.*
Trade or trading: *cheat in a business matter.*
Trading, bargaining: *business prosperity.*
Train, riding on: *matters develop quickly.*
Train station: *unexpected visitors.*
Trap - door: *unexpected good fortune.*
Trap, seeing: *wickedness will be clarified.*

Travel - bag: *a long trip will soon take place.*
Treasure of tremendous value, finding: *death or shame.*
Treasure, to own or discover: *betrayal by your best friend.*
Tree, falling down from: *loss of job, favoritism and prestige.*
Tree-garden, seeing: *riches, great wealth.*
Tree, old one harvesting fruits: *inheritance receiving.*
Tree roots, seeing: *becoming ill, sick.*
Tree, seeing green and in full bloom: *joy, unexpected pleasure; happy marriage.*
Tree, seeing a dry one: *means death.*
Tree, seeing yourself in, high up: *power and honor.*
Tree, sitting under: *good news is coming.*
Tree, split by lightning: *separation of two lovers.*
Trees, fallen, destroyed by lightning or burned in half: *annoyance, fear, anxiety, pain, despair.*
Trees, on fire, burning: *family quarrels.*
Trees, logging: *means misfortune.*
Trees, picking leaves or fruit: *casualties; losses; illness.*
Trees, with lots of fruit, seeing: *profit; wealth.*
Trees, without leaves, seeing: *finishing business transactions.*
Trip, making: *avoiding vexation.*
Trousers, seeing: *error, mistake.*
Trout - fish, seeing in water: *cheer and love will enhance your life.*
Trumpets, hearing: *reunion or astonishment.*
Trumpet, playing: *hoping for employment.*
Turkey - bird, seeing: *being freed from a miserable situation.*
Turkish - people, seeing: *laziness will hurt you.*
Tulips, many beautiful ones: *changing your living standard.*
Tulips, having in your room: *coming into better conditions.*
Turnpike: *all kinds of obstacles coming your way.*
Turtledove: *unshakable love and friendship.*
Turtle, eating: *reaching your goal after putting forth effort for a long time.*
Turtle, seeing: *you cherish a secret joy.*

U

Udder of a cow: *blessings; gifts.*
Umbrella, seeing: *means, caution.*
Umbrella – sun umbrella, seeing or using: *finding support; recommended by sponsors.*
Undressing yourself: *bad news.*
Uniform, polished, wearing or seeing: *promotion, great honor.*
Uplifting, seeing yourself: *great honor.*
Urinating: *disagreements.*
Urinating, wetting the bed: *clarification in confused matters.*
Urine, drinking: *having a lot of expenses.*
Urn, seeing: *danger ahead.*

V

Vail, wearing: *respect and love.*
Vampire: *sliding into the influence of a swindler.*
Vase, with beautiful flowers: *gaining wealth.*
Vase, breaking: *losing your boy- or girlfriend.*
Vat - tub, seeing filled with wine: *good income.*
Vat - tub, full but cannot be used: *death in the family.*
Vegetables, raw, seeing or eating: *troubled business; annoyance; sickness.*
Vehicle - car, a nice one: *coming in contact with nobility.*
Vehicle - car, riding in: *prosperity.*
Vehicle - car, sitting in the backseat: *bad gossip.*
Vehicle - car, seeing turned over: *imminent casualties* <u>experiencing</u>
Vehicle - car, stepping out of it: *loosing your position; or dignity.*
Vehicle-wheel: *embarrassment experiencing.*
Vein, huge one, seeing: *a scare about your heart.*
Velvet: *haughtiness, arrogance brings you down.*
Vending machine, seeing: *profitable business.*
Vetch, flower: *your modesty wins over new friends.*
Villages, seeing: *attending a merry, joyful gathering.*

Villages, seeing in prosperity: *indicates happiness.*
Villages, poor, visiting: *losing respect; experiencing disdain; contempt.*
Villager, seeing or talking to: *happy days ahead.*
Vinegar, drinking: *annoyance; dispute in the household; disagreements.*
Vinegar, making: *your mind reflects about evil things.*
Vinegar - red, seeing: *misused; abused; deride.*
Vinegar, seeing: *being offended.*
Vinegar, spilling: *being disliked; accepted with skepticism.*
Vineyard, walking through: *prosperity; happy family; accommodating friends.*
Violets, not yet in bloom: *lawsuit, losing friends and estate.*
Violets, seeing in full bloom: *rewarding efforts.*
Violets, seeing in summertime: *wealth and honor.*
Violin, seeing: *pleasant company.*
Violin, holding or playing: *calmness; patience; unpleasant situation.*
Viper, seeing: *lucky in love, great wealth.*
Visiting someone: *injustice enduring.*
Visitors, expecting: *uncomfortable situation ahead.*
Vomit, yourself: *for poor people* - *good omen;* **for rich people -** *disadvantage and damage.*
Vulture - falcon, seeing: *malicious illness.*

W

Wafer, seeing: *a wished for message, receiving.*
Waffle: *your thirst for pleasure brings harm.*
Walking alone, being lonely: *changeable luck.*
Walking and hesitating: *losses and obstacles in business.*
Walking, constantly: *careful in your approaches.*
Walking fast: *taking on a task without hesitation.*
Walking with friends: *stability.*
Walking with your lover: *unstable relation.*
Wall, collapsing: *misfortune for you or in your family.*
Wall, in front of you, seeing: *annoyance and struggle.*
Wall, jumping down from: *joy and fun.*

Wall, standing on: *huge success.*
Wall, surrounded by water: *coming into disgrace.*
Wallpaper, seeing: *joy-bringing news.*
Wanderer - traveler: *forthcoming trip.*
War cry, vengeance: *happiness; prayers and wishes are being answered.*
War armament: *very bad omen.*
War, going to: *conflict with your superior.*
Warehouse, being in it: *betrayal openly exposed; pursuit.*
Wart, seeing: *malefactor gets you in trouble.*
Washbasin: *cleanliness is the foundation of health.*
Washing, seeing: *libel, slander.*
Wasps: *unpleasant involvement.*
Watch, a pocket watch: *good omen.*
Water, seeing bright and clear: *prosperity; happiness.*
Water, seeing calm and cloudy: *life is in danger, illness.*
Water, warm, drinking: *rejected by friends; sickness.*
Water, walking through: *rescued from danger.*
Water, having over you: *advantage.*
Water, walking on it: *flourishing success.*
Water, in a broken glass, running through: *being dishonored; losses; bad luck.*
Water, pure, clear, being offered in a glass: *soon to be married; happy childbirth.*
Water pail: *unpleasantness will disappear.*
Water mill, seeing or being on it: *happiness, wealth, honor.*
Water snakes: *recovery — of the ill and sick.*
Water, roaring and sweeping: *bad luck on trips.*
Water, being pushed into: *grief and worries.*
Water - nymph, seeing: *treason, prosecution.*
Water-can, seeing: *do not go into extravagances.*
Wax, seeing: *be patient and wait, victory is yours.*
Weasel, seeing: *malice will harm you.*
Weaving, mill seeing: *lots of luck in speculative operations.*
Wedding, seeing: *jealousy, lingering disease.*
Wedding, having: *enduring damage.*

Wedding, marrying a woman when your wife is still alive: *confusion in your plans.*
Wedding, attending and seeing dancing: *means a suffering heart.*
Wedding, attending: *joy and good news.*
Wedlock: *prosperity, happiness.*
Weeds, seeing: *enduring losses.*
Weeping: *losing a friend for a long time, sorrow and grief.*
Weeping, to see someone: *comfort.*
Wellspring, seeing with clear water: *a sincere confession.*
Well, strong current: *danger of fire.*
Well, bathing in clear water: *escaping from danger.*
Well, seeing in beautiful architecture: *receiving nice gifts.*
Well, falling into: *in fear of the future.*
Well taking water out: *prosperous business deals.*
Whale: *huge disaster.*
Wheat, seeing: *effort leads to prosperity.*
Wheat field in bloom: *wealth and honorable love; all wishes coming true in marriage; many well-mannered children.*
Wheel or wheelwork, seeing: *forthcoming illness.*
Wheels, turning: *quickly reaching the goal you hoped for.*
Wheel of fortune, seeing: *misfortune or annoyance.*
Wheelbarrow, being pulled by dogs: *despair.*
Whet-stone, seeing: *good results in trade.*
Whey, drinking: *worrying about your health.*
Whip, seeing: *beware of punishment.*
Whip, swinging: *making friends through honesty.*
Whistle, trying to, but can't: *obstacles in your plans.*
Whistle, hearing: *warnings about something.*
Whiskers, having on yourself: *idle, transient joy.*
White grouse, flying: *unexpected news.*
Whore, seeing or talking to: *happy days ahead, luck.*
Whorehouse, seeing: *misfortune; pursuit; sickness.*
Widow, being: *receiving satisfaction.*
Wife, talking to: *unstable changes in business.*
Wig seeing: *vanity brings sorrow.*
Wind, a cool breeze: *good events; joyful news.*

Window, at the rear side of a building, on fire: *losing close relatives.*
Window, at front, on fire: *death of a relative or acquaintance.*
Window, climbing out: *bad luck in business.*
Window, seeing open: *happiness in your household.*
Window, seeing closed: *means they coming down hard on you.*
Window, you falling out from: *means lawsuits.*
Window, stepping through: *being accepted positively, friendly.*
Windowpane, seeing: *complicated situation.*
Wine, spilling: *losing respect.*
Wine, seeing: *hemorrhage - warning.*
Wine, drinking, good taste: *showing resistance.*
Wine, mixed, drinking: *illness or changing luck in business.*
Wine soup, eating: *indisposition.*
Wine, getting drunk: *receiving love and respect from a noble superior; happiness in the future.*
Wings, having and flying: *"good" for everybody.*
Wire, plain, seeing: *traps being set.*
Wire, made out of copper: *profitable, lucky, ongoing business.*
Witch, seeing: *being involved with a greedy person.*
Wives, seeing many: *change and variations.*
Wolf, biting you: *slander; libel.*
Wolf, killing: *getting rid of a bad, tricky enemy.*
Woman – whore, being in her company: *gossip; inconstancy.*
Woman, being favored by them: *arguments ahead.*
Woman, clothes, wearing: *sorrow, misfortune.*
Woman, courting: *being cheated by flatterers.*
Woman, fooling around with: *dispute about inheritance.*
Woman, having more than one: *being tormented.*
Woman, old with white hair: *losses of many kinds.*
Woman, beautiful, being in love: *happiness, health and wealth.*
Woman, seeing pregnant: *good news.*
Woman, seeing with beautiful, long hair: *honor and wealth; happy union.*
Woman, seeing with black hair: *uneasiness and sorrow.*
Woman, seeing with brown hair: *means illness.*
Woman, seeing with red hair: *being pursued.*

Woman, unknown, seeing or talking to: *acquaintance.*
Wood, cutting: *diligence and progress.*
Wood, carrying: *becoming poor.*
Wood, logging: *means death.*
Wood, picking up or piled up: *grief, a lot of affliction.*
Wood – picture frame: *great honor.*
Wood, throwing into the fire: *waste; extravagance.*
Wood, floating on water: *devastation of your longed-for happiness and love.*
Wooden shoes, seeing or wearing: *modest, but happy family life.*
Wooden vessel, seeing: *modesty prevents starvation.*
Wool, buying or selling: *luck in business, good income; respected by noble authority.*
World, ending: *stupidity creates obstacles.*
Working: *a good continuation in ventures.*
Worms, seeing: *careful — evil surrounds you.*
Worms, killing: *being set free from drawbacks.*
Wound – sore, seeing or being wounded yourself: *good prospect in projects; harmony in the family; false friends are giving up on you.*
Wounded person, seeing: *your lack of consideration means disadvantage to others.*
Wreath, carrying: *take the salute.*
Wreath made of myrtle: *means a wedding.*
Wreath making: *diligence.*
Wreath, by a funeral, or grave: *inheritance, or loosing your loved ones.*
Wreath, woven from evergreens: *fulfillment of your hopes.*
Wrestle: *quarrel and dispute.*
Wrestle with a beast: *defamation.*
Wrestle with a stranger: *imminent danger.*
Wrinkles in your face, seeing: *reaching an old age.*
Writer, in an office or public office: *a confusing situation.*
Wrought iron, making: *dispute, argument.*
Wrought iron, seeing or being hit: *great losses.*
Wrought iron, seeing red-hot: *intimate love; high blood pressure; nervousness.*

Y

Yard, seeing messy: *disparage.*
Yard, backyard, spanning a net, like a roof: *great wealth.*
Yard or farm, your own: *rich inheritance.*
Yarn, entangled: *lovers chasing each other.*
Yarn, unwinding: *prone to lavishness, to discover a secret.*
Yarn, to rewind: *becoming greedy.*
Yeast, eating: *prolonging physical sufferings.*
Young, becoming: *vanity causes heartbreak.*
Youth, seeing a young man: *only through your own strength you will reach prosperity.*

Z

Zebra, seeing: *don't befriend fools.*
Zero numbers, seeing: *riches, wealth; honor; good fortune in ventures.*
Zither, playing: *pleasant appearance in society.*

Nostradamus Egyptian Dream Interpretations 1928

The End

Nostradamus Original Dream Book published in 2003

www.nostradamusdreams.com

THE NEW MILLENNIUM

Revolution In The Cosmos Revolution Here On Earth ....

... coincidence or consequence?

A true visionary or prophet can never be wrong.
Those who are privileged to foresee, receiving prophecies, must have the ability to understand and comprehend The source of inspiration, which radiates in enlightenment has its divine origin. The superiority and simplicity of the Cosmic Laws, bearing the Will of the Creator/God are stunning and guarantee strict and equitable justice in all the Spheres.

Nostradamus writes in his foreword to a letter to King Henry II of France:

"It is true Sire, that I inherited from my ancestors the talent of seeing into the 'future', but I do not imagine that I am the only one who can foresee. I connect my 'natural talent' with my astronomical calculations and bring them together into a uniform whole picture.

"I free my SOUL, my SPIRIT and my HEART from all worries, doubts and false moods and silence my thoughts. Then, when the LIGHT surrounded me and GOD spoke in IMAGES, it was not myself but the DIVINE LIGHT that spoke through me!"

Enlightenment through intuitive perception, as we know, is like an infusion of Divine –Spirit in communication concerning future events ahead of time, when being in tune with this pure conception of the radiating Spirit-Energy, which streams like a beating pulse throughout Creation and is connected with all living forms, including the human beings felt by our Soul/ with the core of Spirit. These facts lead us to the recognition of the operating cosmic principal Law of *"cause and effect --- what you sow you will reap," which reveals the greatest knowledge we humans can attain." / as Abd-ru-shin points out Author of "In the Light of Truth."*

Nearly 450 years ago, Nostradamus, the great astronomer and astrologer, pointed to a specific date, August 11, 1999, when an extraordinary planetary constellation would take place. He remarked the date, which heralded the beginning of the New Millennium, as the *"Turning Point for Mankind"*. History's great Seer made us aware of this unique event in the Cosmos and its decisive significance for the future of humanity and planet Earth.

Have we again ignored these signs of celestial warnings?

When the 9/11 events unfolded, according to Nostradamus the episode constituted a "test" and also to see how the USA and the world would react and in which way they would retaliate.

Turning point for mankind means a turnaround from the previous ways of dealing with conflicts in the world, to avoid the consequences that would thereby ensue according to universal law. Two World Wars not long ago, suggest that no lessons have been learned from the past.

Nostradamus foresaw in his quatrain:

(Centurie VI / 97)

"Like an earthquake, fire from the middle of the ground, shakes the new city and its surroundings. Two big concrete blocks engaging in a long war. Arethusa will color a new river in red."

The "new city" is undisputedly New York. Two concrete blocks are the "twin towers", giving rise to a long war, which is still raging more than a dozen years on and with no end in sight.

"Arethusa" is the name in Greek mythology of a nymph living on the island Syracuse. What is remarkable is evidence of Nostradamus' high inspiration and intelligence with a coded name *"Arethusa"* in precisely denoting location of events hundreds of years to come.

Areth means Earth in Hebrew – he was of Jewish descent – and the remaining letters *usa* describe with a certain precision where the decisive events of 9/11 would take place, on an "Island" (Manhattan in USA); the consequence of a long war giving rise to a flow of much bloodshed he named: *a new river in red.*(*terrorists around the globe*)

The next Quatrain further confirms the one before: Quatrain: (Centurie VI / 97)

"The sky will burn on the 45 Latitude. (New York) The fire will be near the great New City. Sky high sudden flames shooting up, in an attempt to 'test' the Normans."

Nostradamus called Americans *"Normans"*, amazingly. He was only 11 years old in 1492 when Columbus was officially recognized as the discoverer of America. But unknown at the time was a *Norman of Groenland* who had reached the American continent around the year 1000 AD, as would later be documented in history much after Nostradamus' time.

The total sun eclipse that occurred on August 11, 1999 was regarded as the last in the twentieth century. It plunged first the United States into darkness, followed quickly by Europe, and then the Far East, where it was culturally perceived as a "bad omen". In contrast, we in the Western Hemisphere were enjoying it, seeing in it nothing more than a sensational spectacle in the sky.

It was indeed a warning sign for the human race, indicating that events of severe devastating proportions were imminent. Nostradamus gave us this warning for the New Millennium, documented in a letter to King Henry II of France. His concerns were mostly addressed to governments throughout the world, and in his own words:

"If world leaders, heads of state make wrong decisions, these subsequently would have terrible consequences for humankind and bring on environmental disasters on earth."

What have we witnessed since then?

Visionaries never know the exact time when their vision will become reality. Nostradamus could have merely recorded what he saw and left things at that. But out of concern for the generations to come and to match the time frame as closely as possible, he used his mathematical device (laid down by a divine cosmic code he unlocked). He was able to inform us of planets repeating stellar constellations or aspects, as would recur on August 11, 1999 (with the planet Mars, from Mythology known as the War - God, was in closest proximity to the earth in a long time). He warned us of the significance of that date.

But reading warning signs from the stars is not something man takes seriously, otherwise we could have prevented the subsequent senseless sufferings around the world since the year 2000 owing to wrong decisions by world leaders. The knowledge of the up-building Cosmic Laws, the Laws of Creation, is required to combine the earthly and the otherworldly <u>domains</u> beyond matter in a uniformed interaction, which leads us to understand "reality" in its completion; something which science still struggles to accept.

What have we, in fact, seen since August 11, 1999? The US is at war and the whole world is walking on dangerous tightropes. The Far East shudders with ingrained tensions, and the Middle East is imploding, fermenting a revolution. Terror spreads – some would say, rules – across the globe. As if human misbehavior was not enough, natural disasters strike hard in all corners of our planet, almost daily. Fires rage wildly, destroying vast areas and conurbations in many countries. Floods keep on wreaking severe devastation around the globe, with no end in sight. Draughts persist in the USA, Canadian prairies and Africa. Volcanoes erupt more frequently and earthquakes more powerfully than ever before. Hurricanes and tornadoes reap through the US in increasing severity, causing vast devastation. And in 2004 Mother Nature unleashed the most devastating power of destruction in the Indian Ocean "tsunami." (Remember the total sun eclipse in 1999 appearing in these affected regions of the planet *as a warning sign,* yet ignored and dismissed by the majority as superstitious nonsense and unimportant?)

According to Nostradamus, atomic and biochemical warfare is imminent unless our political leaders see the wisdom of adopting a more gentle approach to solving international conflicts with which our planet grapples. ***Retaliating with force to smother the cries of the victims of injustice will, he says, result in "World War Three".***

At this point we can only say that once again, as always with his predictions, he was right in seeing ahead the world situation of today. But why do we not prevent the dire warnings from manifesting into reality? *It lies in our hands alone to do so!*

We and not the Stars determine our destiny always, each individual one exclusively can contribute for the common good. The stars and their radiations do not create or invent our fate or karma. *As agents of execution*, they can only attract and condense ripe karmic forms and channel these back to their authors, whether individuals or an entire nation. Not that the intervention of the stars in our lives is proof that we are not free; rather *the stars are only vectors of the "living Justice of our Creator/God".*

"*Human justice seeks to* **punish** *– Divine justice wants to* **educate!**"

Although mocked as a *"doom seer"*, Nostradamus, however, had no wish to terrify with his predictions but only to *"warn"* of the inevitable. If our politicians and heads of state act appropriately, putting concern for human welfare before political gain and expediency, further devastation can be eased or prevented, and indeed, this is the purpose of a prophecy. We have the knowledge and recognition of the governing Laws also known as Natures-laws, we have to honor and respect, including the law of *"cause and effect"*, *"what we sow we will reap"*. But if we do not respect but rather ignore these perfect self-acting Laws that affect all of us, *nobody can then escape the ensuing consequences that WE ALL MUST FACE!*

Adapting to a more humane and respectful international relations, is one way that will diffuse and not exacerbate tensions around the globe, thus away from what has so often happened in history and still today.

In our self-acclaimed arrogance we continue to ignore the orderly structure laid down by law's of the Creator's blueprint, showing HIS Will expressed in Nature's basic rules. To adapt to her great and noble simplicity, which we must learn to understand in order to engage in rightful behavior, is to preserve humanity and prevent the disintegration of Planet Earth all together.

We have available the complete knowledge of Creation. Our coming-into-being and how the interwoven self-acting Cosmic Laws operate, and how they give form to the material reality of lives, are explained fully in the book "IN THE LIGHT OF TRUTH" by *Abd-ru-shin* (Oskar Ernst Bernhardt).

This knowledge enables us in our time to heed Nostradamus's words for the New Millennium – the ***Turning Point*** he foretold –

"renewal of man and -- spiritual awakening" …..

in order to achieve the 1,000 golden years on Planet Earth as predicted..

PLANET EARTH---MOTHER NATURE

"Human Beings temporary home"

The world we live in, from the recurring seasons, the daily sunrise and sunset, is a repeating cycle, an essential part of Mother Nature's designed operation. We have rightfully given Nature the name "Mother". She indeed provides for all her inhabitants the requirements needed to live here on earth, together with the "renewal" or "rebirth" we witness every spring.

A wave of joy reverberates throughout Creation and resonates in human hearts when in spring the season of new growth arrives together with the first signs of life, for example, in the form of a small bud appearing on a naked branch or a new sprout from a planted seed that sneaks through into the sunlight for the first time. We also share this wonder of new life in jubilant joy, often taking it for granted.

So, too, does the human species, which is likewise subject to Nature's Law, need to awaken the spirit-kernel within, need to awaken our living core of being which distinguishes us from all other creatures and "crowns" us among all life forms on earth.

With this responsibility in mind towards Mother Nature and also our fellow man, the picture would look like this:

We enter this world as a baby *(like a little rosebud on the mother's stem)*, with a core of implanted spirit-germ forming the basis of our personal identity. *Mother Nature takes care of the little rosebud by providing rain and sunshine essential for growth, so that one day it will mature into a full grown rose in its true identity, then wither as the life-span comes to an end, until a new cycle of life begins in the spring again.* This repeating life cycle Mother-Nature operates in accordance with the Divine Will of the Creator/God

This metaphor applies also to us humans:

The loving care fostered by our biological mother "from day one we are born" sets the stage for our entire development, both physically and foremost for our precious soul in growth and stability. Tears and laughter (like rain and sunshine for the little rosebud), *joy and sorrow, are essential elements on our life's journey for maturing inwardly, essential for our spirit to develop into a self-assured personality with noble conduct and beauty, our true human identity, which life's experiences help us to achieve.*

In the autumn of our years, the crown of our blossom when wisdom sets in with the inwardly registered values collected during our life's journey, we accept the approaching day of passing, thus being called "homeward" from the earthly plane into the eternal world, toward *the permanent home of our spirit, which is Paradise.* One life cycle ends, and at the same time a new spirit incarnation in the womb of a "mother-to-be" is taking place, welcoming another human life to begin its journey here on earth again.

We also witness the events every fall in nature's repeating cycle of continuation when the ripe fruits fall from the trees, making room for a new beginning in the spring. That is a manifestation of a deep-rooted interwoven repeating pattern running like a heartbeat through Mother Nature's organism, interconnecting us with a continuation of "rebirth and death".

Have you ever sat in a garden on a calm morning hour, observing the undisturbed purity and beauty only Nature can present and an overwhelming joy fills your heart? It is no wonder, because the beauty of her images has since ancient times served poets, science and Nostradamus in his dream knowledge as the universal language in communication between the invisible beyond and the physical earthly domain. The author of

" IN THE LIGHT OF TRUTH ", *Abd-ru-shin*, gives the following guidelines:

"There is only one Power of our Creator, which streams through all that exists, animating and furthering it!

"This pure, creative Power of Light flows continually through the whole Creation, lies in it, is inseparable from it. It is to be found everywhere: in the air, in every drop of water, in the growing rock, the struggling plant, the animal and naturally also in man. There is nothing where it would not be."

We must finally acknowledge the fact that our beating pulse (spirit) is connected with Nature's powerful spirit- energy radiation, her heartbeat and therefore we must adapt to her united activity. To jeopardize these foundations by continuously trying to alter her operating balance would also destabilize our habitation, as Nostradamus already warned of the consequences 500 years ago. Adapting to her "natural beauty" in a co-operative manner is like an invitation for us to live in harmony and peace—and in true humanity what *would radiate from within us and would thus not allow any evil attentions to take hold.*

Take for example a tall green tree in its majestic appearance, producing the oxygen we depend upon to breathe, which we take for granted. It serves a purpose, as everything here on earth is for a purpose. *Every human individual soul has a purpose to contribute in part to the whole.* What if some day Mother Nature stops providing us with what is so essential for our existence and one we take for granted? Have we ever in our so-called busy days sent up a *thank you* to the heavenly provider?

When birds join together in a chorus of jubilation greeting the arrival of a new day, it gives the impression that Mother Nature's creatures are expressing gratitude. This is expressed *so naturally* to the dispenser, the everlasting Divine Spirit-Energy at work and feeding the heartbeat throughout Creation. And what about us, what about our daily thank you? Having no time is our excuse, being too occupied with the computer and TV?

Just by observing the tranquility of Nature for a moment before rushing out at daybreak to our not so inviting offices in the grey cold stone buildings of our cities, can do wonders for us. By breathing in Nature's simplicity of purity and beauty will echo from within and a sun-filled day for us and around us will unfold. . Watching the bees for a moment busily visiting blossom after blossom, at work extending their morning kisses to set in motion a new cycle of fruit-bearing, we take it all for granted for the most part when biting into a delicious fruit and have almost forgotten who was at work and *so naturally* fulfilling their dutys! Such little contributions one might think, big deal; but seen from a different perspective, they have *such huge effects for us all, and touching our Soul* . Watching these activities of Mother Nature's little helpers for a while, being of service so naturally, deep gratitude should pass through our heart in recognition of the Nature's provision that we take for granted, yet so many hardly notice. This alone should be a reminder of life's values, and the sun would always shine for us even on rainy days, reminding us of how worthless it is to let ourselves unnecessarily be consumed daily by self-inflicted stress.

Without experiencing the sun in our heart, or tears of gratitude, the language of our soul that we try to hide instead of letting them flow, thus suppressing an important element that is necessary for our personal spiritual growth, we will never achieve the mature inner peace and wisdom we can strive for *so naturally.*

Do we give thanks for our daily food, or teach our children to honor the daily bread we take for granted? Should this not come *naturally* everyday and not just once a year at "Thanksgiving"? It seems we have neglected and almost forgotten what values we can learn from Mother Natures provision being granted and provided by our Creator for his creatures on planet earth.

Why do we not start our day so positively, silently thankful for being alive, for our health and for our daily food provided, (we take for granted, but is it really?) so that we can take part in the turning wheel of life around us, joyful and in gratitude everyday. Should this not come so *"naturally"*?

When we touch base daily with Mother Nature's harmonious rhythm, this sets us automatically in harmony **within** and our constant complaints will disappear, which only take hold in an empty, unfulfilled person we identify as being "unhappy".

We alone through our willingness and inner strength can gain self-assurance, resulting in a positive outlook on life, as we can witness daily with the little inhabitants demonstrate *so naturally, --------and letting us smile.*

As a Chinese proverb affirms:
"The smile you send out, comes back a thousand fold."
Nobody would struggle anymore, feeling like a "worthless sense of being alive", which today is a trend increasing at an alarming rate especially among our youth. Many turn to drugs to silence their inner emptiness, because there is nothing solid inwardly worthy to hold on to, and abusing alcohol to dull the pain is a kind of a escape rout of not having found their self-worth and purpose in life is not the answer to the problem. To find that, we have to dig deeper into ourselves and to recognize God the Creator in the ***Universal Love***, acknowledged and observed in the beautiful vibrant radiant essence presented in Mother Natures untouched beauty seen around us, we are part of and belong to, which we should adopt and can hold onto. This streaming Light--Power of Love, like threads hanging from above and around us and available equally for every human soul to connect to and draw from *in our own personal way, would grant humanity to achieve Peace on Earth!*

"Be the change you wish to see in the world!" – as Gandhi reminded us.

The natural goodness of universal love felt within is from the same source as the animals draw from and connect to when expressing affection to us humans, like an interplay of genuine love of all creatures universally ***bonding us.*** This kind of feeling, of being touched by, where the mind is not interfering, has the healing power of *"nourishing empty souls"* and will eliminate any emptiness or worthlessness felt within a human being and you will happily rise to your actual "self " again.

Cherish the gift of being alive, find your place and purpose so that you can be part of a useful link in the chain of the turning wheel of life that you are so important of and only ***blessings will find you in return***. Keep in mind: ***Every individual alive is here on earth for a purpose, otherwise he would not be here.***, (by Creators-Will)

Discover your true "self ", contribute in a caring, loving way of service; join the entire family of humanity, regardless of what you do, and the reward you will earn is *"everlasting inner peace".*

Are we derailed and disconnected from our natural roots what is of Spirit ?

There are millions in our society presently whose so-called scale is not balanced. They struggle to find refuge in nighttime of sleep in order to restore the inner balance. The mind, operating as a tool in interaction with the spirit, creates the balanced scale of harmony in us very ***naturally.*** Even if dependent upon all kinds of advertised pills that promise uninterrupted sleep and unfortunately with the attendant endless side effects, destroys our natural way of staying "balanced". We have become uprooted from Mother Nature, the substance of our material embodiment, and have forgotten where and how to find the source and cure for our overall well-being., laying dormant in us waiting to be actively awakened.

Every artificial external help interferes with the healthy operation of our bodily organism and thereby can also hinder the necessary opening of intuitive channels foremost during our time of sleep, when the pure strength to nourish our soul can flow freely so that we are *"recharged", **from the powerful infusion of spirit-nobility,*** otherwise we block the interaction from happening altogether.

Waking up miserable in the morning, having missed out on a qualitative sleep and for example feeling weak and not fit to take on a new day, because they feel not up to doing anything, they wonder in their self pity and pessimist outlook why they have no luck, joy or happiness in life. Starting a day in fear and insecurity brings us nowhere. Keep in mind that we alone are in charge and set the tone to have a sunny or cloudy, a positive or negative day.

Belonging to the family of all the living which Mother Nature caters for, only man, the highest developed species, can no longer hear her language, which is our *"inner voice"*, the expression of our *"ego or self "felt and heard by our Soul from within.* But instead relying mostly on artificial drugs to silence the body imperfection, we have to deal with the seemingly never-ending consequences of side effects after disrupting our organism in its natural activity, being thrown out of its natural balance.

Have we ever seen an animal walking into a drugstore? It follows mother nature's voice in its natural instinct, which guides it to the appropriate herbs to cure bodily discomfort, by Natures care provided, as the Chinese culture has acknowledged over thousand of years and successfully practiced ever since. And what is the highest developed species "man" seeking?

No man-made pharmaceutical products can replace nature's herbs in perfection. The whole of nature with its diverse healing power provides the appropriate remedies to keep our body in good health in the first place.

The question may arise how should we understand "being natural". *Natural means striving upward, like being pulled by an attractive power towards the eternal 'Light', like every blade of grass, every flower, every tree does "naturally" in striving towards the sunlight.*

To follow those simple rules and just being *"natural"* in everything we do is like striving upwards to our *"Eternal Light" the home of our spirit/Soul helps us to achieve.* Paying more attention and listening to our inner voice, carrying goodness in our heart, there lies the greatest challenge for our own well being and our responsibility towards our fellow man, for preventing planet earth from further disintegration from what is seen everywhere at present time and Nostradamus already made us aware of 500 years ago.

In creating a more friendlier atmosphere in our immediate human conduct throughout the world by everyone's participation in humanity, we in return, through the self-acting Law of *"sowing and* reaping", "cause and effect", will earn only goodness and blessings, joy and peace as an everlasting reward–*that is the Law*.

None but our very self, the human spirit, equipped with "free will" in decision making, is always the master of its own destiny. If he strives to be of good volition so as to understand the purpose of his existence and fulfill his mission in Creation, then everything will come to his aid; everything, including stellar radiation, *"The wise man masters his stars".*

The great philosopher J. Wolfgang von Goethe's famous maxim states: *be careful what you wish for, because one day you must deal with it."*

Wow.........what responsibility lies in this fundamental statement by divine Law for us, showing us the reciprocal action ? It takes away our comfortable escape route in blaming our failure on others rather than seeing it as our own fault.

We see these laws in action *as consequence* everywhere, in our personal life when we take a closer look, or in a larger picture of world events created by our governing leaders and our general acquiescence. We can see these effects everywhere and cannot escape but must face them, there are no other exceptions because it is

"The self-acting Universal Law, which we must learn to understand, respect and must also fear." – Abd-ru-shin

Nature is living proof that we are all under a unified, perfectly operating "higher Law". For example: putting a carrot seed in the soil means we "must" harvest carrots. There is no other option and nobody can ever change these facts.

That is natures Law.

When we call into a forest "ugly", the echo we hear will also be "ugly", and even if we wish to hear "beautiful" it never will happen.

That is the divine Creation Law.

When you keep your thoughts pure, only directed to good intentions, you will earn only "goodness" in your life in return.

That is the self acting Law in Creation.

If in business you trick your partner in an unscrupulous manner in trying to gain an unfair advantage, you will have to deal one day with the consequence of failure or misfortune by the Law of "reciprocal action".

That is the Law.

Nature and her laws demand motion in everything and punishes those who disobey the simple laws. God does not punish men as many people imagine. Men punish themselves. Our Creator has no need to interfere, to punish or reward, because HIS Laws are so perfect that they do all the work for HIM. It is the Divine Laws which " Judge" man and his activity !

True simplicity at its greatest !

What is man's lifeline ? It is the Truth Christ brought for all men irrespective of race, color or creed. Truth is for the individual. The individual has to work his passage through life on his own. Nobody, no religion, can do it for him.

The path is being offered one more time to humanity in an understanding of the 21. century. It is the continuation of Christs bringing WORD 2000 years ago, layed out in finest detail in the **'Grailmessage** */ " Tn the Light of Truth'. /by* **Abd-ru-shin**

Be reminded, complacency is the enemy of spiritual seeking !

It is only through understanding and living Truth that we can fulfill our true purpose and in so doing, return to Paradise---the home of the Human-Spirit.

This shows us the *"key"* we hold in our own hands, in our private life,, in business and for the whole world affairs, to create and shape our private and a entire nations future, in creating their own destiny. Now you may ask what is this universal energy operating in Nature's Law?

A testament by science, the famous Physicist Max Planck/ Germany,1918 Nobel laureate, acknowledged long ago:

"The invisible immortal spirit – radiation is the essence of existence, generating and sustaining life."

It is this invisible material of "Radiating Light-Power --- which the astronomer

Nostradamus acknowledged also (500 years ago) as radiating through planets and stars.

It is this invisible "Power" moving in cosmic forces that he recognized to be of immense influence in our everyday life, in the past, today and in the future, and also influencing our nightly sleep.

It is this invisible "Energy of Light" which feeds our mind during the day, in perceiving our intuition–our inner voice–and is the silent language of symbol-images seen in a dream.

Therefore, when incorporating this living power of "divine Light" into our plans and deeds of our every day life, we will automatically shape our own destiny in the best way possible.

" I have *lived* what I wrote."! Therefore I can give testament to the **Truth.**

God is the Power that activates Natural Laws;
the Power that nobody has yet grasped or seen,
but whose *"effect"* everyone must see, if he only
chooses to do so.

-Abd-ru-shin

EPILOGUE

Nostradamus' enigmatic name followed me all my life in fascination. His fame has lasted more than 500 years and will outlive many generations yet to come.

When I conducted my research in Europe, finding the reason why such a rare Nostradamus book of dream-knowledge could have disappeared and also be declared officially "lost" by the National Archives was quite astonishing.

There was a time period, circa 200 years reaching into the twentieth century, when writings and documentation associated with the name "Nostradamus" were forbidden in public circulation. Many of the valuables left by him were confiscated and destroyed, lost forever.

The reigning monarchs, world leaders and church authorities who had great political influence then took such drastic measures and desperate actions and they knew the truth of cosmic influence. They feared that if the public were to learn an outcome coming true from Nostradamus' accurate foreseeing and not according to their intentions, their dictatorial grip would be undermined and victory would not be on their side. They were very well aware of a higher power guiding events, but self-involved dictatorship as always dominated and succeeded. After World War II, writings by Nostradamus started slowly surfacing again in private, and his *"Egyptian Dream Book"* was among them.

I followed my inner voice to revive his lost work of dreams, I inherited and preserved it from extinction. I felt I owe homage to this wise man, and as I now know, acting on sheer intuition like a link in a chain, *in destiny's decided time period at the beginning of the New Millennium, after 500 years of his time on earth, as it was pre-*

dicted by the seer himself when his given "knowledge " from long ago can take hold and be fully understood.

Nostradamus predicted;

Quatrain (Centurie III / 94)

*For a long time my work was not understood,
nor accepted, rather ignored
But 500 years from my time on earth, in that New Millennium
Great clarity will come about.
And through my legacy, mankind's happiness will prevail.*

Quatrain (Centurie III / 2)

"The Divine Word of Truth" (Grailmessage) will give mankind the opportunity to understand heaven and earth in their interconnectedness. A human –being has everything under his feet to walk on, as he would be in heaven."

Looking back at historical documentation, traces left from high civilizations that have survived to the present day we only know as *"myths."* While details may have become blurred with the passage of time, the traces at their core indicate **knowledge and application of never-changing Divine Laws**. This quality ensures their survival, because their nature is beyond the limitations of space and time and partakes of eternity. *And this very nature is the essence in all the works of Nostradamus* left for us long ago, and so little we have understood.

500 years ago only the privileged had access to higher knowledge; not so anymore, the time for a "New Knowledge of Creation "is here now and it is available for the entire human race, in over 80 countries and in over 25 languages available.

DISCOVER THE HIDDEN TREASURES OF SLEEP!

The GRAIL MESSAGE
Original Edition from 1931
» IN THE LIGHT OF TRUTH «
by ADB-RU-SHIN

**Answers to Questions
That agitate the human soul!**

This unique classic work of Natural-Science - Philosophy explains the world, and how the Natural – Laws work in Creation. It addresses all of man's unanswered fundamental questions of life and therefore in a logic clarity guiding us to the *TRUTH*. It was already known to my grandfather in 1933 and my entire family since. It became my Sword and shining Light throughout my life. I am ever so grateful for this guidance to the *LIGHT*.

Dita Arzt-Wegman
http://www.abdrushin.us/in-the-light-of-truth/
This is the original edition from 1931

The divine father / God has laid the power of his spirit for everything already in us human beings - YOU only have to make use of it.
- Abd-ru-shin

The tragedy of life is what dies inside a man while he lives.
- *Albert Schweitzer*

ACKNOWLEDGEMENT

Only if we strive earnestly to understand the interwoven rules and regulations in Creation, the expression of the Will of the Creator/God in His "self-acting Laws" operating universally and thus also for us transient guests on earth, will we succeed. These laws of reciprocal action provide the guidance to achieve our highest goals during our life time---------and thereafter.

The "Divine Master" (Creator - God) laid down the railway tracks for us human beings. The destination of the rolling train we are riding on our life`s journey is predetermined for every traveler, by divine Will. We humans are bestowed with a *"free will"* and can choose in which coach, economy or first class, we want to ride on our journey. Through exercising our "free will" we choose and decide our direction—leading upwards to the light, or downhill. Through pleasant or unpleasant experiences arising from the nature of our interactions in daily life is serving our own goal leading us closer towards our Spirit to mature.. We alone decide for ourselves, and therefore carry alone the responsibility for our actions, for which we will one day be held accounted for.

We can, if we wish, jump off the predetermined laid out tracks on our journey, but as long as we never lose sight of the train in motion and keeping in mind always the hope of still reaching one day our end destination in the best way possible.

We find in the moving train –coaches for every traveler various menus of guidelines displayed to choose from for all those who intend following the set path in reaching the final destination one day according to the plan of the divine "Master's Creator/Gods Blueprint" laid out for everyone.

Do we not all hope for the best journey possible until the last station is reached? How can we be sure of our arrival if we so often deliberately deny, mostly through willful ignorance, *'the Knowledge'* we are provided with of how to get there?

Only making the effort to understand the Creator's *"travel guide"* as contained in the *"Message from the Grail –* IN THE LIGHT OF TRUTH" by **Abd-ru-shin**, (Oskar Ernst Bernhardt, 1875-1941), which bridges the gap between belief and conviction, will get us there. It will assure staying on track and avoid missing the connecting train that awaits each traveler at the earthly terminus, the end of earthly life when we must journey into the world beyond. The transition of "changing trains" you may experience as bumpy or smooth, depending on the experience and quality of lasting values acquired, which helped us to " mature our Spirit" No action, word or thought is lost in the Cosmic Book of Life, but everything has been registered to our name and to our personal account held, by God's accounting department of his self acting laws – like a computer's stored-away personal data.

Either way, the next train will see our journey continuing through realms with more beautiful landscapes. The way to make sure of that is to follow *our inner perception of the "travel guide"*, laid out in the Living Word of Life:

Find Your God
"God is Life"
"IN THE LIGHT OF TRUTH"

Abd-ru-shin

ABOUT THE AUTHOR

Dietlinde (Dita) Arzt was born in Sudetenland (Bohemia). As a little girl she experienced with her family the atrocities of war, even after the official declaration of the end of World War II.

Her father's abduction by the Czech and Russian invaders and all man from the village where transported as prisoners to Siberia. The left behind family where then helpless in the hands of the brutality of Czech and Russian partisans. All families from the entire village had only two hours time to gather at the sports field, and surrounded by soldiers and at gun point where forced to flee on foot day and night into neighboring Poland. Deprived of their estate and the traumatic scenes experienced from this exodus left permanent mental scars in a little child's soul as a painful permanent imprint.

The expulsion from her beloved homeland and the estate that had been in her family's possession for over 250 years, is to be found in history books as:

"The 3 Million Sudeten-Germans, a human tragedy of injustice", documented as the *"Other Holocaust".*

Miraculously her father survived 2 years of imprisonment in a Russian labor camp. The remaining family survived the horror of war, and with the help of the International Red Cross they were reunited in Germany in 1947, having thereby returned to their ancestors roots of origin, which can be traced as far back as the year 1228.

Dita has always been, and remains still today, intensely grateful to her parents for having not only provided a loving and caring home, which made you feel being 'protected', for her and her two sisters, Gertraud and Dorit, one not measured by material means since Germany lay in ruins, *but for demonstrating excellence of character and profound inner strength, and thereby planting in her the seeds, so vital for any young life, of the stability essential for all future personal growth.*

Dita's decision to "explore the world on her own" made her leave her protected nest called "home" and moved to Munich. She started as an apprentice in a trading company, when she came in contact for the first time with Nostradamus' Dream Book. Many great opportunities opened as she also pursued the career of her dreams as an actress and model. She enjoyed her success but preferred to continue in her business career. Progress in her profession required her to travel internationally, and her destiny brought her to Canada, where she married and started a family. In addition to raising two daughters, Dita and Cora, she climbed the ladder of the corporate world. For twenty-five years she held the position of vice-president of an international cosmetic company.

But not enough, advanced in years she again tested her gifts in the entertaining business as actress and model in Toronto.

Retired from the business world, Dita has now dedicated her time to her long- standing literary interests to delve into and expose life's meaning and purpose.

She has devoted her first writing to share with the world the last remaining *"Dream Book" by Nostradamus, preserved in 2003 from extinction.* It is widely extended in her latest book *"Discover The Hidden Treasures of Sleep".*

I am certain that fate has afforded me to preserve the "Knowledge of Sleep and Dream", showing no separation between this world and the beyond. Dreams and visions are meant to help make contact with the extrasensory, I am privileged passing it on for future generations.

1503----Tombstone of Nostradamus-----1566

I was privileged to be among the visitors from around the world who in 2003 commemorated the 500th anniversary of Nostradamus in Salon-Provence, France. I visited his tomb in the Collegiale Saint-Laurent paying my respect. It was an unforgettable moving moment, bringing home his lost Dream Book, revived and preserved from extinction, as my gift in his honor.

On the 2nd of July 2003

IMPORTANT QUOTATIONS NOTED THROUGHOUT THE BOOK FOR DEEPER REFLECTION AND FURTHER CONSIDERATION...

1) Our true ego is Spirit it is the only living thing within this earthly body of ours that keeps us alive as such.

Dag Hammerrskoeld - Secretary General of the United Nations 1953 - Nobel Prize for Peace 1961

2) The purpose of human earth-life is the development of the human spirit, from the subconscious being, becoming a self-acknowledged personality!

3) For that to achieve is the earthly daily interaction in all 'life's' field given extensive opportunities to experience.

4) 'Knowing' and getting to know only derives from experiencing life.

Albert Einstein

5) To be rich in spirit, is the same as 'having deep inner feelings felt by our Soul, but not the same as being highly intelligent.'

6) Those collected valuables of ours are being imprinted forever in our Soul/Sprit. Are your own jewels stored away (by divine law)?

7) Emotions are the expressions of our Soul-Sprit, becoming alive, being stirred up again and tears are the expressions, felt from deep within.

8) The small brain-cerebellum is assigned (by Gods-creators of his creation) as a bridge staying connected with the home region of our Spirit/Soul (beyond).

9) The frontal brain is only in charge for our daytime activities.

10) We must finally give our Spirit-Soul its assigned 'master position' back and let our mind be the servant, our tool, in order to succeed in the right direction, whatever we do.

Abd-ru-shin, the Author and messenger of "IN THE LIGHT OF TRUTH"

11) Every illness has its roots in the mental condition of ours!

12) The day shift comes to an end and the night shift begins for all life forms on planet earth (by nature's law). Giving human beings time to 'recharge our inwardly faculty, for us to have restored the harmonious interaction between Mind and Soul to start refreshed our new day in the morning'. That is the actual purpose of WHY we must sleep.

By the Author Dita Arzt-Wegman – 'Discover the Hidden Treasures of Sleep'!

13) Natures images we see in our dreams are the universal language of our Soul, the bridge in communication from the extra sensory to the physical world.

14) What happens when we die? Medical standpoint - the shell, our human body is without the energy-power of Spirit, it has left its earthly presence, we call death.

15) Transmission from the earthly domain to the realm of the spirit-origin took place, medical Mystery??? BECAUSE WHAT THEY CAN'T TOUCH NOR SEE, THEREFORE CAN'T EXPLAIN WHAT IS TAKING PLACE, BY ITS' BRAIN LIMITATION only BOUND TO THE PHYSICAL.

SCIENCE IS ONLY ANALYSING WHAT ALREADY EXISTS, BUT NEVER REACHING THE FUNDAMENTAL CORE OF ITS' ROOTS (you find all explanations to these questions and so much more in the classic work 'IN THE LIGHT OF TRUTH' WHAT ORIGINATES FROM A HIGHER PLANE THE SPIRITUAL REALM BEYOND.

Science has finally to step over the physical boundary into the next level of existence, to have and to find answers to their medical questions of life and death and so much more.......read more in the book.

16) Is it arrogance or ignorance not to accept the findings from their very own long ago when Physicist MAX Planck 1918 openly acknowledged:

The actual, the Real, the True, is not physical transient substance, but the invisible, immortal Spirit.

Max Planck - Germany - 1918 Nobel Prize winner in Physics

TESTIMONIALS / BIBLIOGRAPHY

Oskar Ernst Bernhardt / *Abd-ru-shin*/ Germany
1875-1941 --- Grail Message - In The Light of Truth

Max Planck - Physicist / Germany *Nobel Prize 1918*

Albert Einstein—Physicist / Ulm – Germany
Nobel Prize 1921

Manfred Eigen—Natural Science / Germany
Nobel Prize 1968

Gary Zukav—Physicist / USA

G.C Lichtenberg—Physicist /Author
-1742 / Germany

J. Wolfgang v. Goethe—Poet, Philosopher, Author
-1749 / Germany

Herman Hesse – Poet/Author / Germany
Nobel Prize 1946

Alexander Solzhenitsyn / Russia
Nobel Prize 1970 in Literature

Masaru Emoto – Japan / Researcher
"The Message of Water"

Michel Nostradamus---Astronomer *1503—1566* / med Doctor/ France
Sleep, Soul and Science

APPENDIX

A BOOK FOR ALL THE WORLD
IN THE LIGHT OF TRUTH
...the Grail Message - of Abd-ru-shin

Abd-ru-shin
(Oskar Ernst Bernhardt,
his civilian name)
1875-1941
Author of -
IN THE LIGHT OF TRUTH

A special book, which clearly answers the unsolved problems of human existence. The vast knowledge mediated in its pages leads the earnestly - seeking reader, who weighs and examines objectively, out of all the chaos of the present day confusion and distortion, to clear recognitions.

This book commands attention by its forceful language, by the clarity of its thoughts and by the setting right of distorted concepts, unmistakably and sometimes severely but irrefutably explained.

The laws in which the entire Creation came about into being and exists are plainly set forth, the World happening is interpreted in its true significance, and man's responsibility before God and his fellowman is revealed and explained. Thus to him who opens himself to these recognitions is restored the indestructible inner security of his personality.

In the 1920s and 30s Abd-ru-shin wrote with his Grail Message **"In the Light of Truth"** a unique work concerning all the fundamental questions of our life.

Original Edition: German
Translations available in: Arabic, Czech, Chinese, Dutch, English, Estonian, French, Hungarian, Italian, Persian, Portuguese, Rumanian, Russian, Slovak, Spanish.

Obtainable from the book trade and Grail World contacts.

Dr. Richard Steinpach/Author
1917 - 1992 Vienna/Austria
The Author draws his
knowledge from the
'Grailmessage'
In the Light of Truth.

WHY WE LIVE AFTER DEATH
ISBN 1-57461-005-8

WHY WAS I BORN?
ISBN 1-57461-003-9

HOW CAN GOD ALLOW SUCH THINGS?
ISBN 1-57461-009-0

**Nostradamus'
Lost Egyptian Dream Book**, 1928 rediscovered, preserved from extinction. Published at his 500th Anniversary Year 2003.

by Dita Arzt-Wegman
Available in:
Arabic, English, French, German, Italian and Russian.
www.nostradamusdreams.com

Discover the Hidden Treasures of Sleep
is my newest book----it is your living key on your lifes journey ------ for happiness and success.

1503 - 1566
Michel Nostradamus

NOSTRADAMUS HIS LIFE AND LEGACY

He walked the earth 500 years ago and is still known in every corner of the globe. His fame has not diminished because his accuracy in predicting future events fascinates us now as it has always done, and always will.

Who was this enigmatic man really?

Should we not ask ourselves from where he drew such knowledge, a knowledge of events hundreds of years ahead?

Could this have been other than that he was gifted to allow us a glimpse into the future?

Is it possible that he was privileged and perhaps chosen to provide mankind an invisible but very effective source revealing "what lies ahead"?

Could it be that the pattern of events is predetermined by divine power shaping the destiny not only of the world but of all human beings?

Or do we determine our own future and create our own destiny through the fundamental Natural Laws, including the law of "sowing and reaping / and cause and effect"?

For those who have never heard of "Michel Nostradamus, 1503-1566", I would like to mention only one remarkable story. One day, when passing by some monks walking on the side of a road, he instantly fell on his knees and kissed the robe of the most humble monk. When asked why he was doing such a thing, Nostradamus replied: *"I must kneel before his Holiness."*

Forty years later and 19 years after Nostradamus death, the same monk became "Pope Sixtus the V".

All documentations concerning Nostradamus are displayed in his museum, a tourist attraction in Salon Provence, France, where he lived his last 20 years with his family until 1566. I was privileged to have attended his 500th commemoration on the 2nd of July 2003. Visiting his tomb and bringing home his "lost Dream-Book", revived and preserved from extinction as my gift in his honor, was an unforgettable experience.

Ancestry

Michel de Notredame was born on December 14, 1503 (according to the Gregorian Calendar in his time; the actual date is December 24 in our present time) in the small town of Saint-Rémy-de-Provence, France.

He grew up in privileged social circumstances.

His father held the office of Notary, and married into the noble house of St. Rémy's. His was a very educated family with a vast knowledge of literature, history, medicine and astrology. His maternal ancestors were renowned physicians. They were famous doctors who served in royal households. The passion of Nostradamus' maternal grandfather, however, was not medicine but exploring the mystery of celestial bodies. It was he who introduced the young future seer to the activity in the cosmos and the powerful driving force of a Universal Law behind it from a supreme source of the Highest Order, the Creator.

Members of this remarkable family maintained close contact for generations with wise emissaries from the Muslim Arab civilization that flourished in neighboring Spain and was then, in so many ways, far ahead of Christian Europe. Not only medical and philosophical but also magical lore suffused the culture. It was an opportunity to come in contact with ancient knowledge, magic and medical wisdom. Exchanging the experience of healing power in herbs, the popular "folk medicine", proved very effective in the years to come when the plague, known as the "black death", raged in southern France.

Michel in his young age preferred gazing at the stars. He inherited the fascination with this unknown domain of the Universe from his grandfather, John de St. Remy, who spotted the zeal in young Michel's curiosity to know more about the secrets of stars and planets and with delight he passed on his findings. He introduced and taught young Michel astronomy and astrology. He explained the laws of the universe, and guided him to an understanding of the purpose served by rays projected from constellations of stars and planets, which determine events occurring here on earth and influence human behavior.

He showed great interest in astrology and celestial science, a fascinating subject in his time, but the decision to follow in the footsteps of his family to study medicine took priority.

Medical Career

At age 14 young Michel set out early for the University in Avignon, France, taking on the family tradition in studying medicine. He passed the medical examination in 1529 aged only 26, which was an astonishing achievement then. Now as a young doctor, just in time it seemed to take on the plague ("Black Death"), which was passing through his region. Most of the population fled the cities in fear, including his fellow students and university professors.

Michel did not flee. Armed with courage and determination and what we can only assume was an extraordinary inner drive, a source little known at the time and as mysterious as the medical knowledge he possessed, he took on the fight by himself. His use of simple hygiene, fresh water, clean linen and fresh air was the basis of his success in fighting the plague. This groundbreaking procedure was instituted in the later medical practice and is still in vogue today. No one knew then of bacteria, viruses or antibiotics. But Nostradamus, whether acting out of sheer inspiration from knowledge bequeathed by his mother's family of famous physicians, or information obtained from his neighboring Spanish-Arab contacts, no one knows how his knowledge of the use of a certain combination of herbs came about that he gave his patients to chew on. This procedure stopped the further progress of the disease, and his courageous actions alleviated the suffering of so many.

He was celebrated as a hero among his people. His reputation traveled fast and laid the foundation for him to become one of Europe's most famous personalities.

Nostradamus thereafter opened his own medical practice, married and fathered two children. In addition to his spectacular talents, he was a devoted family man, amiable and good natured. His people treated him as a respectful dignitary, but he preferred the image of a humble, friendly citizen, and always enjoyed a great sense of humor.

A couple of years after, Nostradamus closed his practice and followed his restless urge to travel, to further explore. He started his journey on horseback to various countries, visiting different cultures. He consulted and exchanged experiences with doctors to learn more about the healing power of herbs. He traveled, as history documents, a great deal through Europe and North Africa.

But his travel came to a sudden end when France, foremost the region of Provence, where Nostradamus lived, was plunged for the second time into the most horrifying "plague". Those who remembered Nostradamus when he defeated the Black Death before searched for his whereabouts. They located him in Italy and brought him back home, where he found his wife and his two children among the casualties of the terrible deadly disease.

He worked for three years, 1546 to 1548, as a doctor in the city of Aix, fighting to defeat the plague again, and he succeeded a second time. The news traveled fast and reached the Paris Court of King Henry II, who summoned him to Paris to thank him personally for his tremendous achievements.

(It was the same king whose death Nostradamus later accurately predicted.)

A friendly relationship was established from then on between the Royal Family of

France and Nostradamus, which lasted for the rest of his life.

Astronomy and Astrology

A mind such as Nostradamus' is bound to be restless and constantly questioning, inquiring into matters of the fine spiritual and coarse worldly. He thought about things other people dared not to think about or explore, even if they could do so. Nostradamus would go so far as to seek out the very driving force of the universe itself.

The seeds once planted by his grandfather, to explore the cosmos with its mysterious activity, had germinated into growth.

Absorbing much of the metaphysical lore concerning the correspondence between the high and the low led him, after using his mathematics, to acknowledge a driving force of the highest order. These governing "Universal Laws" known to science form the principle by which the stars and planets move in precisely repeating patterns, as well as the whole activity in the cosmic world. This Light-Power (Energy) has now finally been acknowledged by modern science as an *"consciousness energy"*.

As the famous physicist Max Planck publicly acknowledged:

"The Actual, the Real, the True is not transient substance, but the invisible, immortal Spirit – in Radiation."

The mathematical system by an astronomical devise Nostradamus used helped him to calculate time and position of the planets. He used it later as a kind of time frame for predicted earthly events. The influential rays of a stellar constellation are not just a spectacular event in the universe but should be seen as an indication like *a prelude of what is to come on "stage earth."* The consequence of an occurring constellation can be seen here on earth as a visible effect in Mother Nature's acting behavior.

What distinguished Nostradamus from his predecessors was the ability to place foreseen events in a certain time period. He recognized a governing Law based on a mathematic law, an occurring repeating cycle, and came close to a certain time period when events will occur.

He found it essential that the radiation pulsing through the planets and the entire universe maintain order and balance, supporting and influencing the existence of all life form on earth.

Astronomy, the royal art mastered by Nostradamus, is perhaps more than ever recognized by science today as evidence of a wisdom and inspiration worthy of being called "divine." He achieved great insight into the relationship between the material discoveries of man and the laws of the world beyond matter. He understood that the world of matter itself depends on the eternal world that is beyond space and time, and should therefore be recognized as a manifestation of "Truth".

Armillary Sphere: Astronomical Device, 1594.

The philosophical basis of his dream interpretation went beyond the sages of the ancient civilizations of Egypt and Assyria, who studied the celestial bodies exclusively to obtain valuable information and guidance on the predictive power of "dreams" by humans. He uses the same basis of dream knowledge that was established by the ancient cultures, which the Greeks and Romans later continued to build on. Relevant documents exist in the British Museum in London, England. Nostradamus extended that knowledge through his own research and visionary insight, and bestowed us with his work known as "The Egyptian Dream Book."

The Seer of the Future!

After marrying a second time, Nostradamus settled with his family, including 6 children, in Salon, France, where the family lived for the next 20 years.

At the age of 44, in 1547, Michel Nostradamus began documenting his predictions. Already a famous celebrity, his fame grew even more with the requests of the nobility for their personal horoscopes.

The French Queen, Catharine de Medici, was a great admirer of Nostradamus. He had warned her that her husband would be killed if he took part in a duel, but the king dismissed the warnings. The opponent's spear pierced through his eye and brain and he died an agonizing cruel death on July 1, 1559 just as Nostradamus had predicted.

After King Henry's death, his son and successor Charles the IX made the now extremely famous seer Nostradamus his personal astrologer and physician. It was commonplace at that time for a ruling monarch to have frequent recourse to the services of astrologers, and to follow their advice in the timing of important undertakings, including when to go into battles. These reliable sources made victory most certain.

In 1555 Nostradamus compiled his collected visions, the result of his nocturnal rituals. He described the process of his meditations thus:

"When the Light surrounded me and spoke in the universal language of images, it was not me, but the Source of the Highest Order in purest Light-Radiation that communicated through me."

Among his most remarkable predictions for our time and in regard to events on this continent are:

- The assassination of John F. Kennedy
- Man's landing on the moon
- The collapse of Communism
- 9/11, attack on the Twin Towers in New York City

Also remarkable is the beginning of the New Millennium / 2000, which Nostradamus named:

"Turning-point for Mankind"!

He did not base the coming events pointing to a single person, leader or dictator, but he addressed the involvement of *"all the world leaders"*, as though he was aware that 500 years from his time on earth there would be a body established as a *"United Nations"* to solve conflicts by consensus.

(Invading Iraq by the US was without the consensus of the United Nations, which the world still has to deal with today with its terrible consequences.)

Many who have studied Nostradamus and his predictions are of the opinion that more than half of his prophecies are about events that are yet to occur.

Nostradamus arranged his visions into 1,000 quatrains, 4-line verses. They were later published under the collective title, CENTURIES. One of the most famous, pointing to the present time, is Quatrain:

Quatrain Centurie X / 72

Unanimously interpreted as referring to August 11, 1999 (using the Gregorian Calendar current in Nostradamus' time).

The content of this prophecy, referring to a King of terror, Planet Mars (is known as the War-God), coming from the sky, is such that many astronomers and astrologers from around the world had asked themselves if it meant the "end of the world"?

In consideration of the tremendous tension generated by the exceedingly rare disposition on that day of the Sun, Moon, Mars, Saturn and Uranus, forming a square (solid line) and in addition they faced each other in direct opposite, (interrupted line), it was feared that this portended destruction, geological or otherwise, for the human race. The only hope remained in the constellation of the positions of Venus and Jupiter (solid white line).

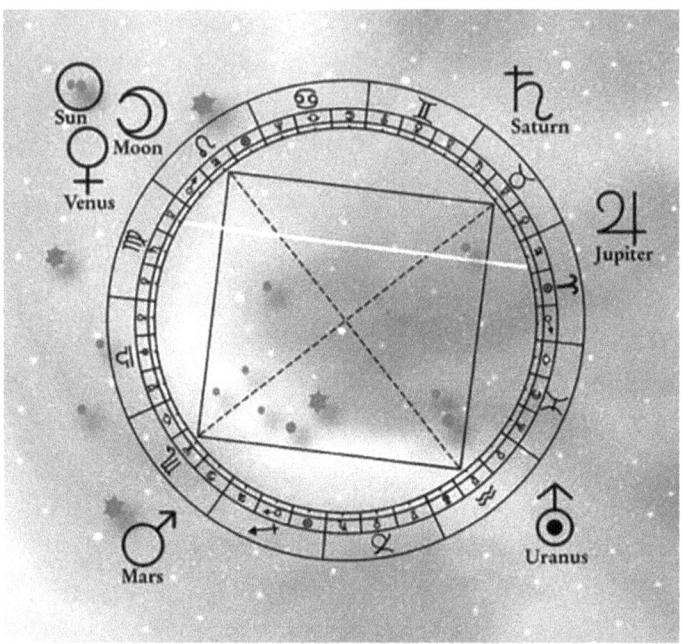

As we all know the world did not end that day, as many had feared.

Sensational media and even Nostradamus interpreters included, tried to exploit it as proof that Nostradamus and his prophecies were and are false. And so they preferred to revel in their own imaginings about its significance. It never occurred to them that "Nature's self-acting Laws" operate differently (as the wishful thinking of little men anticipates) and at a different pace from what we would like to see in our imaginations.

In order to be able to grasp the significance of this prophecy and to understand the true meaning of this date, it is necessary to have knowledge of the immutable lawfulness of nature. While events on our earthly plane are guided by radiation of the planets in their particular characteristics, holding us in the tides of their pounding influence, the visible manifestation of the effects takes time, not measured by our means. This process is based on the fundamental law of "cause and effect", which is interwoven like a thread through all that exists, and under a different dimension of time.

Nostradamus foresaw his own death.

Shortly before Nostradamus died, Queen Catharina de Medici traveled with her sons to Salon and took residence in the Chateau de l'Emperie. The entire royal family, admirers of their personal physician Michel Nostradamus and personal astrologer, paid their respects once more, not knowing it would be their last meeting when inviting him to the castle which was only a 5-minute walk from Nostradamus' residence. He conducted a physical check up on everyone and also predicted that each son of the Queen would one day wear the crown of France.

And so it happened as history has documented.

Not long after, Nostradamus had spent an evening chatting with another close friend and confidant, de Chavigny. Before his guest left, Nostradamus remarked "goodbye my friend, tomorrow morning at sunrise I will no longer be here. De Chavigny, needless to say, thought he was joking, as was often his nature, and therefore did not pay much attention to his remarks. The following morning, however, Nostradamus, on arising, experienced severe chest pains, sat down on a bench next to his bed and collapsed. It was in July 1566.

Nostradamus had foreseen the exact circumstances of his death, and recorded these words:

"There is nothing more to be done. I am entering the eternal world. Next to my bed, on a bench, they will find me --- dead!"

It was exactly how he was discovered.

Years later, in a small calendar found in his jacket, next to the date July 2th he had placed a mark and inscribed the Latin words,

"Hic mors prope est. ---- Death is near."

What more compelling verification could there be of the fact that the "Truth" is to be found revealed in numbers and symbols, imbedded in the superiority and simplicity of Cosmic Law.

A Selection of Nostradamus' Prophecies that have come true:

July 1, 1559
The French King Henry the II is wounded in a duel and dies 10 days later.

January 30, 1649
The English King Charles the 1st is beheaded.

Summer 1666
London is burning. The announced plague is the punishment for the murder of the king.

1804
Napoleon marries the daughter of the Austrian Emperor.

August 1846
Discovery of Planet Neptune.

April 20, 1889
Adolf Hitler is born in Braunau, Austria

1936
Franco in Spain divides the Spanish nation, and civil war follows.

1938
Hitler marches into Austria.

1939
World War II starts – 290 years after the beheading of King Charles the 1st.

1945
Hitler's death after the wedding in the bunker in Berlin.

1948
The State of Israel is established.

1954
Abdel Nasser establishes the Arabic Republic (UAR).

1979
Victory of Ayatollah Khomeini over the Shah of Persia.

1990
The End of the Soviet Union.

1999
War in Kosovo.

2000
Turning Point for Mankind.

2012/Dec 23 / Cosmic – Shift, / New Age of Aquarius begins.
…..Renewal of Man….Spiritual awakening!

2020 Corona Virus

Nostradamus made this prediction in the year 1551 – coming true now.

> He predicted:

> *"There will be a twin year – 2020 – as we know now from which will arise a queen Corona who will come from the far-east (China) first and will spread a virus/a plague into the darkness of men, and also on a country with 7 hills (Italy-Rome) as we know now and will transform the **twilight** of men into dust (death) that will ruin the world."*

All predictions from Nostradamus starting from 1559 came true and not one could have been proven wrong over centuries. Because they were obtained by Gods will and executed by his self-acting laws, ruling creation and planet earth showing us the outcome, the effect we must deal with, what is imbedded in the beating pulse of planet earth and all inhabitants and man included. Humans are the leading part in it since we are the only specie bearing the spirit core in us, crowning us from all other creatures on earth and therefore connecting us with the realm of spirit which lies on a higher plane, than that to which our earth and we humans belong.

> Nostradamus' own words describing his nocturnal sessions when receiving his predictions for mankind to pass them on:

> *"When the light surrounded me and spoke in images, it was not myself but the divine light – GOD who spoke through me."*

The Corona-virus was produced by Nature with the lined up cosmic influence by stars and planets in their constellation position. This virus was dropped by nature onto the soil in a region of China first as it was meant to be predicted 500 years ago in the plan by Natures ruling lawfulness executed, followed by the country, of seven hills – Italy-Rome as we know now, spreading this virus around the entire globe since.

Therefore the Corona virus was not man made and cannot be blamed on anyone or any country. What little man, in his imaginations, anticipates by his limited brain capacity where the mind limited to matter only can comprehend – what is one sided and wrong.

This plague is only one of many still to come – in the near future *"hunger and starvation"* is the next plague mankind will have to deal with (also predicted by Nostradamus). Since planet earth is overpopulated and Mother Nature with its climate change does not guarantee our natural food we need to grow any longer. As science has warned us also, the planet is in danger. Mother Natures in its orderly ruling is helping itself allowing diseases to occur which will naturally reduce the over population on the planet, in taking care in restoring her functioning balance again.

This is another prediction by Nostradamus:

"The time has now come and Gods wrath of anger is sweeping with an iron broom mankind and when it will be over --- two thirds will perished on planet earth and the third left behind with a renewed human-race will then build up a new earth – restored in its origin of beauty, peace and harmony, the paradise of man as it was meant to be from the beginning of time, will come about."

I want to bring another prediction of a remarkable comet the big star like the Bethlehem-star 2,000 years ago. This special star was filled with high spirit power send by Gods Will to announce the birth of his son Jesus Christ 2,000 years ago bringing the derailed people the word of truth and how they should live by Gods-laws to reach one day paradise in return their home of the spirit after their Life's journey is coming to an end. Today, the same comet is on its way to the earth's atmosphere.

This comet can be called the Bethlehem-star, because it is coming also from the purest spirit realm. It is filled with purest spirit power that has a mission for planet earth and humankind to bring the **turning-point** and **renewal of man** and our **spiritual awakening** to be achieved as predicted.

The characteristics of this star not belonging to the solar system but it is specially sent down to us and will be at the right time appearing on the God given plan to bring big changes by weather catastrophes. This comet has its characteristic to suck water high up what gives everyone when not keeping their eyes shut to see, that he is not far away since the torrential rains and downpour causing floods around the globe in many countries causing suffering and hardships and great devastation.

When Corona and all the other plagues still to come are behind us, this comet is withdrawing his influence leaving his position and taking on the covering of matter for us human beings on earth to see with our eyes in the sky his radiant light. God's messenger filled from the high spiritual power when he is at its closes point to earth, he will with his influence for a couple years surround planet earth to bring about all the transformation as predicted of viruses, plagues so that it will help the derailed human beings getting back on their right tracks again in living by Gods laws what we humans have imbedded inwardly by our spirit presence we feel as our Soul, we hear as our inner voice speaking to us, and is our conscience we should follow in our conduct and behaviour towards our fellow man on planet earth in all we do. After the comet has left its position and influence on the planet, the earth will be cleansed and refreshed in its beauty never before see. The renewed human beings still alive on planet earth will build up our home to the paradise of joy, blessings, and guarantees a bright future ahead for us all. We are one human-race by one GOD who is judging and brings justice to all when not living or obeying his laws as our fundamental base we have ignored over thousands of years and is now our test of survival or disintegration of humankind as predicted into dust/death at the ***turning-point***.

We have arrived at our ***turning-point*** as predicted – *to be or not to be* - and the choice is ours alone. Every individual has to make a decision, staying on the track where we are in far too long leading us further downhill into darkness, or we change course and becoming human-beings again as it was meant since the beginning of time to save our planet, our home, and humankind.

I am compelled to bring Nostradamus' prediction to be understood from the spiritual aspect and for that you must have an understanding and knowledge of the governing ruling laws what moves creation and us humans and planet earth altogether by the will of God/the Creator's radiation of Spirit-power, originating from a higher plane, the home of the spirit which lies higher in Creation than our planet where we humans belong.

Considered leading us to the truth and for that we must have an understanding and knowledge of the governing ruling laws what moves creation, and us humans and our planet earth altogether by the WILL of GOD the Creator's radiation of Spirit-power. It should be our obligation to know and understand these working laws, so that we can adapt to this manifested guidance we see as an example in Natures laws, we can adapt to this fundamentals to orient our own lives and how to live by these laws, since the beginning of time manifested, since we are all under one higher-law all living forms on planet earth, humans included.

But man over centuries and many decades ignored Natures orderly concept by their laws operating, we interfered in her perfect ruling order, disobeyed her laws in their perfection since the beginning of time. The *twilight* of man disobeyed these laws, did not protect Nature in its perfect operation way showing us as an example the right track for our path and how to live by, what should be our guidance staying in harmony with Nature.

As this statement from an environmentalist confirms:

"Protecting Nature – ultimately protects us from viruses!"

We have failed and misused Nature for too long. What should have been our priority ever since and the outcome predicted 500 years ago is now taking effect and Corona is sweeping over the entire mankind affecting and ruining our planet earth, and human beings in it. The effect we see in reality of our own mistakes we have made, we must now pay for by the reciprocal actions, the governing laws in Creation required, is showing us the most severe way of our failure in suffering and hardships we must endure. We must face these consequences, and cannot escape! That is the law shown in Nature as an example, we have failed to protect her, for far too long.

Disobeying these fundamentals, we instead made our own laws and rules as we like them best, left the right track and this derailment we also see in our societies behaviour, not knowing right from wrong anymore is this derailment of ours and caused the *twilight* we are in as predicted and will ruin the world and send humans to dust/death.

Turning point for mankind at the new Millennium *"renewal of man --- and spiritual awakening"* as predicted, what the deadly Corona-plague in conjunction with the lined up cosmos of Aquarius era influence, representing the spirit, enlightenment in support let us to achieve, before we will be destroyed.

Therefore we must change course from our old way where the materialistic orientation by our mind only ruled instead our spirit – what is our Soul – human beings identity in noble conduct should have been our guidance, what comes from within, our inner voice as we know, is our conscience we feel, will from now on be our guidance in our conduct and behaviour, were the human qualities of spirit/soul can be practiced. Respecting our fellow man in loving care around the globe should be our priority. All people occupying planet earth as one human-race are under one ruling law by Creator-God whom we depend on and who let us be on earth in the first place. We have to be thankful and in noble conduct, our human qualities we all bare within us from the beginning of time is evident in our way we live. We must restore all humanity qualities we bear from within by our spirit/souls, we feel from within what is our conscience, our inner voice has to be in our leading master position again what was in us since the beginning of time and not the destructive mind what is only oriented to self gain and superiority over others what leads to hate-killings, in the most destructive way must come to an end now.

By the predictive **Turning-Point**, means we must turn around walking on a new path, leaving the old comfortable way by our implemented laws we followed is our turning point to be destroyed or to be saved, since the planet has also reached its set end-station of existence at present, like all planets in the universe are under this natural ruling – order and transformation when their set time has come to an end. WE see as an example as history has documented, 'the sunken Atlantis-Empire or the Inca civilisation in Peru' – only to name some in history whose existence came to an end, and were wiped out from the face of the earth. And our planet is now also on the brink of disintegration to be or not to be – unless we turn around and try to save it and us human people included before it is too late. Science has warned us many times, our planet is in danger not living in harmony with Mother Nature, nor with our fellow man in respect and loving care, but instead we destroy and kill by our dictating way of ruling over our fellow man instead of embracing them as equal human beings belonging to one Human-Race on planet earth.

Race is not defined by skin-color, but by the qualities of a true human-being we bear within by our Spirit/Soul imbedded as our crown of all species on earth and therefore we are the leaders living as an example in correct conduct what only noble intensions are the goal and caring love rules us is priority in everything we do as a true human-race. WE all must change course entering a new path of living our lives in respect of our human fellow man and loving care. And that is our **"renewal of man --- and spiritual awakening"** required surviving the deadly Corona, or we will be wiped out of our existence altogether, unless we change course. United we can save it from happening in changing course by our different way of life to be lived, in harmony with each other and with Mother Nature is priority can bring us back onto its right track again laid out since the beginning of time and all nations around the globe, united as one human-race so that not punishments we must face by the self-acting laws of Gods ruling order in reciprocal action, we must suffer from in retaliation, but that we can earn blessings instead and not hardships of destruction as we are in right now with Corona and no end in sight.

But we must do the work first in our noble conduct and behaviour in all we do oriented only to the well being of our fellow man on planet earth as One Human-Race in noble intensions practiced is our task to fulfill and could save us from further decline and disintegration altogether, as was predicted for the year 2020.

Otherwise there will be no future for us on planet earth – our home – any longer.

We must adapt to this manifested guidance to orient our own life accordingly and to live by it, since we are all under one higher law we see in operation in Nature as an example to follow, *"what you sow — you will reap"* or the law of *"cause and effect"*. WE now must adapt and bring the human qualities we bear within us by our spirit/soul – our human core and identity to the forefront again to save us and the planet altogether in our conduct to the forefront again, where our noble intensions should be evident, in all we do for us to survive.

> *"God is the power who activates natural-law – the power that nobody has yet grasped nor seen, but whose effect everyone must see if he only wants to do so."*
>
> Abd-ru-shin

But Mother Nature is helping *herself* on its own to establish her lost balanced harmony, man has interfered and ruined her set ruling laws of (spring-summer-fall and winter), to bring back Natures original concept for us to provide our necessary requirements to live on planet earth. Our assigned home on our life journey therefore many thousands will perish from the earth as also predicted by Nostradamus, since the planet is overpopulated ......after we have restored the orderly ruling laws through our behaviour in humanities qualities treating our fellow man around the globe with respect and loving care we must restore. We must do the work first to achieve the renewal of man and to have this planet restored in its original beauty where peace, harmony and happiness will be for all who will still be on earth helping to build the planet up to the paradise for man as it was meant from the beginning of time. And we will stop our abuse, so that in return we will not have to endure more sufferings and hardships, but blessings instead. After we have restored the planet in its original beauty again for our survival by the renewed human beings still alive when all the hardships have passed. By the renewed mankind living on planet earth.

> *"Emotional shocks experienced by (the aftermath of the deadly Corona virus, at present and hunger-Starvation has passed and the climate change affecting us, with the powerful destruction of Nature in full force hitting us and destroying what we have build up – wiped out in minutes, by tornados --- and floods, and raging fires etc. will gradually allowing us to loosen our grip of matter by the intellect, to which also our mind belongs, so that the human-spirit/what is our Soul, we feel from within, is able to understand the language of its GOD again. "*

> *"Death does not have to be feared – death is the REBIRTH into the next higher plane, the beyond – the after-life. Only our body stays behind were it is made of the soil, the earth. But Your core of being is of Spirit and lives on, what is a natural imbedded rhythm of Mother Nature since we are all under ONE uniformed higher – law. Of "renewal --- growth --- and dying."*

Light is always bright shining in purity, by Creators-God designed blueprint in his creation, and we humans are part of, what should reflect in our noble conduct of our Soul as radiant shining-light echoing in our behaviour and conduct. Our Soul with the core of Spirit maintained by our nourishment of believe, in prayers and gratitude in daily life expressed – is our natural build in defence mechanism --- our immune-system as we know what is not of physical substance, but of the invisible powerful spirit in you what gives strength-love and this inwardly maintained strong soil you have prepared in you during your life in daily acknowledgement and expressed, in prayer, thoughts, and deeds does not allow any dark intruders like viruses or illnesses to take hold in you. No evil dark intruders like viruses don't find an equal ground to settle down in your pure prepared Soul of yours, what you have established and nourished during your life, staying strong and healthy in resistance by your inwardly qualities of your Soul with the core of spirit by the law – *"what you sow --- who will reap"* find no ground for viruses or illnesses to settle down, because the resistance is too strong you have prepared in you by the recognition of the powerful material the spirit in strength-love and healing power in protection of yours.

WE must start now before it is too late:

"BE the change you wish to see in the world"

As Mahatma Gandhi reminded us.

The deadly Corona virus with its hardships and suffering is a wake-up call for everyone to recognize the divine power in charge opening your eyes to see whom we depend on --- of *being or not to be* --- *"renewal of man –spiritual awakening"* is necessary by participation of every human soul to decide of letting the planet earth and us human beings go into disintegration, at the set time of the planets **Turning-Point** --- or we change course and save the planet our home and changing our behaviour and conduct practicing humanities qualities towards our fellow man would be one positive step in the right direction – leading us upwards to the shining light.

> *"Embrace this changing transformation you be part of and look upward to the eternal-shining light into the continuation of the* **after-life** *by Gods-Will for all man."*

Appendix page provides more knowledge how to get there ……

IN THE LIGHT OF TRUTH…

The Grail message /by Abd-ru-shin……

In humble recognition of the divine

Dita Arzt-Wegman

(I have lived what I have wrote)

The messenger and author *Abd-ru-shin* of the classic work "IN THE LIGHT OF TRUTH" – the Grail message offers us the way **out of the twilight** by explaining and to understand the working laws in their interconnectedness ruling order in creation and planet earth as one unified whole. Mother Nature as an example is showing us these working laws in matter we have to adapt to, respect and protect. And *Abd-ru-shin* brings from the source of the highest order – GOD the beyond the material behind the appearances from the highest origin streaming down what is the Spirit Power the pulse moving us and sustaining life for us to understand what will bring you closer to your GOD, because GOD is LIFE. No church or religion can bring you closer to him but YOU the individual human-being has every powerful material in him implanted by its spirit you carry and connects you with your God from within, being felt as our soul, is our direct connection with the realm of Gods kingdom – the home of the divine spirit we can reach in our humbleness in prayer every time and every day.

This prayer by the Sioux Indian Chief Yellow-Lark, the nicest prayer ever spoken by millions since 1885 united on a set day, touches the individual which can help you to walk on your new path towards the light, you have chosen:

Laying your humble Soul before your divine father:

GREAT SPIRIT

Whose voice in the wind speaks to me?

And whose breath of life gives to all in this world, --- listen to me.

I come to you, one of your many, many children.

Weak and small I am.

I need your strength, your wisdom.

Let me walk in beauty and let my eyes always see the red and the purple of the sunset.

Let my hands touch in awe-inspiring, what you have created,

Sharpen my ear,

That I hear your voice.

Make me wise, so that I can understand, what you taught my people, seeing in Mother Nature's operation, so that I can grasp what you have laid hidden in every leaf, in every rock.

I seek strength, but not to be superior over my fellow man, but only so that I can fight and overcome my greatest enemy --- my ego, myself!

Make me always be prepared, so that I can come to you with clean hands,

And clear eyes, so that I can come before you without shame,

When my soul one day dwindles, and fades in the lustre and splendour of the sunset.

Make use in your sincerity spoken and blessings will be your

www.ingramcontent.com/pod-product-compliance
Lightning Source LLC
Chambersburg PA
CBHW050740080526
44579CB00017B/81